origami
a-b-c

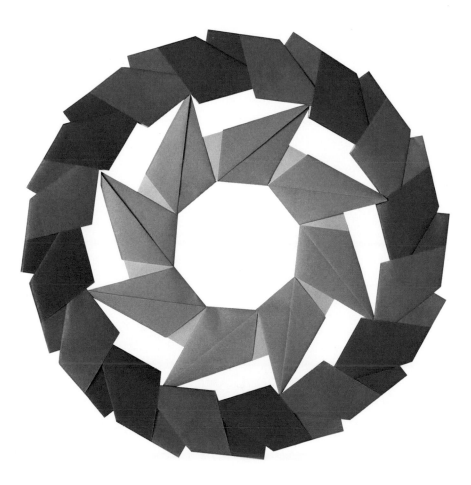

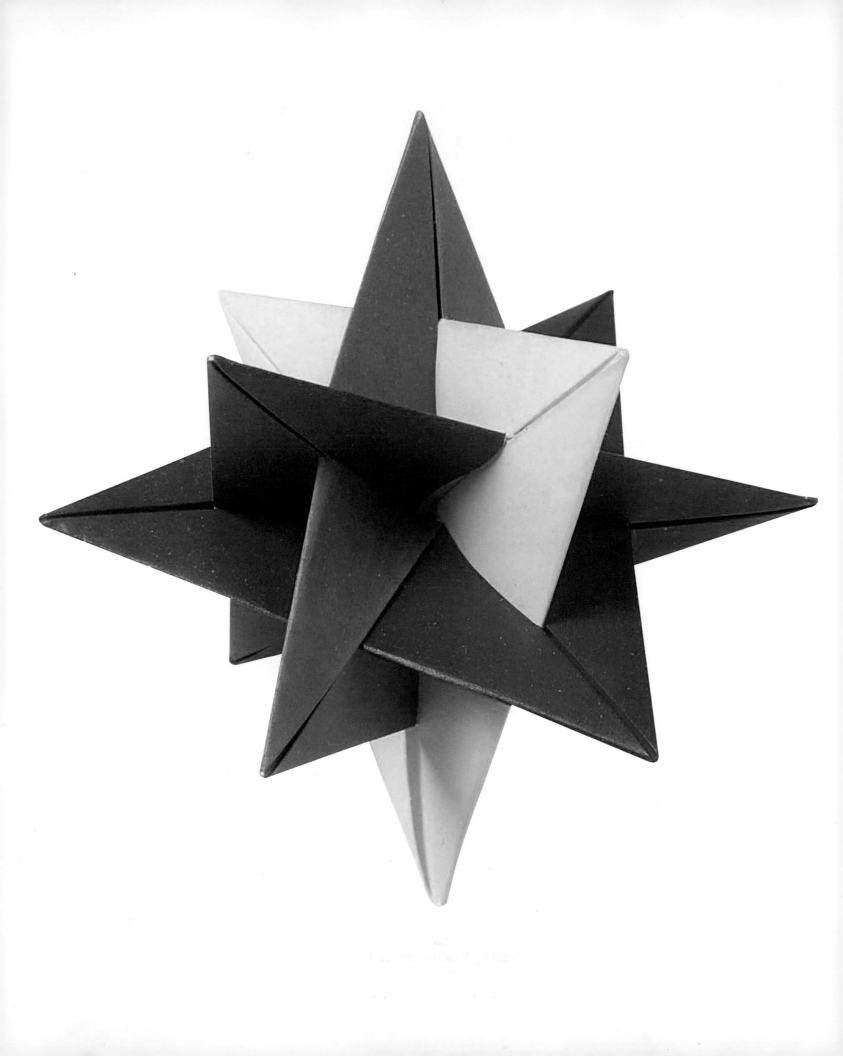

origami
a-b-c

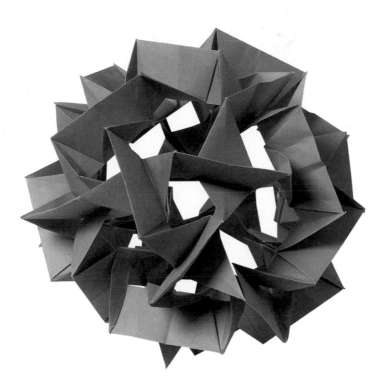

David Petty

Sterling Publishing Co., Inc.
New York

Library of Congress Cataloging-in-Publication Data Available

10   9   8   7   6   5   4   3   2   1

Published in 2006 by Sterling Publishing Co.., Inc.
387 Park Avenue South, New York, NY 10016

Distributed in Canada by Sterling Publishing
c/o Canadian Manda Group, 165 Dufferin Street
Toronto, Ontario, Canada M6K 3H6

Printed in Thailand

Sterling ISBN-13: 978-1-4027-3563-9
ISBN-10: 1-4027-3563-4

For information about custom editions, special sales, premium and
corporate purchases, please contact Sterling Special Sales
Department at 800-805-5489 or specialsales@sterlingpub.com.

Editorial Director: Sarah King
Editor: Clare Howarth-Maden
Project Editor: Judith Millidge
Designer: 2H Design
Photography: Paul Forrester

contents

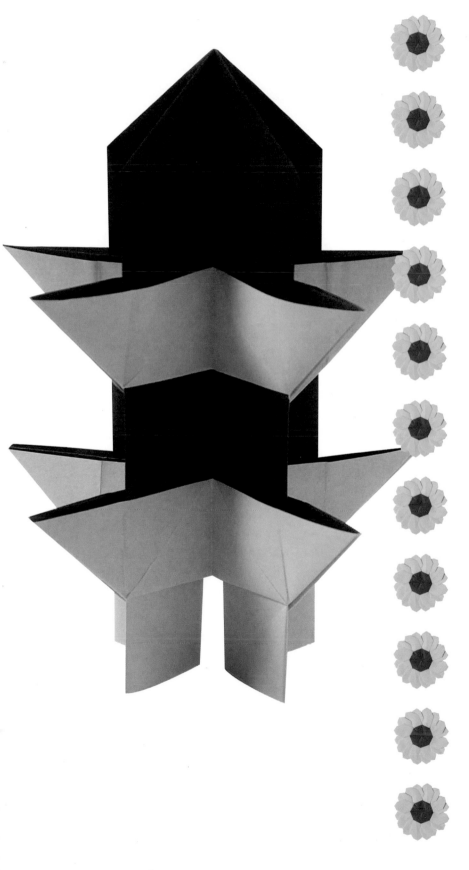

introduction

This book is intended for all origami enthusiasts, whatever their level of expertise. Each origami model has been graded with a a skill level: 1 for simple, 2 for intermediate,or 3 for complex. Beginners are encouraged to work through the book in the order 1 to 3. Old hands may pick and choose at whim.

A few words about the instructions. They must be carried out in sequence, j one leading to the next. Look and read the instruction, understand what is required, then try the fold(s) necessary. Observe and check that what you have done is correct against the next step. Repeat this sequence: Look - Understand - Do - Observe (LUDO) and you will avoid the pitfalls. Look out for "turn over" instructions in the text and also "repeat" instructions. Failure to observe these instructions are the most common mistakes made by new (and old!) readers. Try to be accurate in your folding. If the first attempt is none too good, then fold a second time. Most times, the second is an improvement.

Akira Yoshizawa, widely acknowledged as the father of modern origami, died in 2005 and his passing is a loss to the world of origami. Yoshizawa was responsible for elevating an ancient craft to the realms of an art form. When he first interested himself there were a number of models which were used in religious practice or to amuse children. As the popularity of origami increased in the West, without doubt aided by exhibitions of his works in both Europe (Amsterdam) and America (New York), and the upsurge of general interest generated in Japan, origami (Japanese for "to fold paper") has spread around the globe. There are now paperfolding societies throughout the world, from the UK and USA, to France, Poland, Hungary, Spain, Germany, Italy, Holland, Columbia, Australia, India, Singapore, Korea, and back to Japan.

Origami continues to hold a fascination for mathematicians, educationalists, computer buffs and magicians, as well as children and child-like adults everywhere. The growth of origami societies is no coincidence. Folding can be done on one's own, but is much more enjoyable in company. Fresh ideas develop and help is at hand in consultation with other folders.

In England the rise in origami's popularity was mainly due to the efforts of Robert Harbin, founder of the British Origami Society (BOS). Harbin was an outstanding magician who pioneered a televised series of origami programs. His original philosophy was to encourage two-dimensional models, made from a single sheet, without cuts or glue. This was based on the limitation of sending final models through the postal system. Since then, three-dimensional work has been recognized, as well as folding with multiple sheets. The latter is called modular origami. Its purest form consists of folding identical units (or modules) and combining them with folding alone to make recognizable structures. There are several examples in this book. So the only surviving rules, those of no cuts and no glue, are still followed. These rules differentiate paperfolding from, for example, kirigami (which means "to cut paper") and collage (where paper is glued to a background to form pictures or patterns). At its heart the philosophy of origami is fascinating. Each practitioner has a personal view which may change over the years. Some accept only square starting paper, some fold using only white paper, others allow glue — the differences are many and varied. There is no ruling body which dictates the rules — they only exist inside the heads of the practitioners. Compare this self-censorship with censorship in the motion picture industry. When there were strict rules, directors were very imaginative in depicting sensitive scenes. Once the rules disappeared nothing was left to the imagination and much subtlety was lost. So those who self-impose the strictest rules turn out to be the most creative.

In addition to modular origami, there are several other branches. Money-folding using currency notes as starting paper is popular. Pureland folding is a branch in which only valley and mountain folds are used. The latter sounds attractive, particularly to beginners, but it is now recognized that any model can be made using Pureland techniques — although the folding sequences are longer and more laborious.

Traditional origami normally uses a classical base in the folding sequence (a base is a collection of folds producing a recognized starting point). Instructions for classical bases are to be found in this book. Modern origami employs either a non-classical base or no base at all. There is a rich panoply of styles and techniques all waiting to be discovered and enjoyed.

origami creativity

Introduction

One of the unstated aims of this book is to encourage creators. This page is aimed solely at creation of origami models. Creation of new models cannot be taught. Latent creative skills can be developed. Understanding how the creative process works can help.

The four main creative strands

I have recognized several common threads both from my own experience and when talking to other creators. The following are in no particular order.

1. The improvement ploy

Most creations come from adapting existing examples. In origami terms, produce a variation of an existing model which has different properties. This stems from the idea that the existing can and should be improved. Several times I've seen new models without cuts developed from previous models which had cuts.

2. The creative play ploy

In origami terms, start with a paper, make a couple of moves then see if the shape of the paper suggests part or whole of a model. Make more moves until something is suggested. Work towards enhancing the shape to achieve the final model. With practice recognition of embryonic models becomes second nature.

3. The goal setting ploy

Deciding on a final target then working towards it can be very effective. In origami terms, the final model is decided first, then the most suitable starting point (or points) chosen with the target in mind. What follows must inevitably be the perspiration from the phrase "Creation is 10% inspiration and 90% perspiration." A variation of this ploy is to decide both the overall goal and the starting point, i.e. I want to make a modular piece using a particular base (fish, bird, kite waterbomb, etc.).

4. Serendipity

I define this as the rare occasions when a complete solution springs into mind, almost out of the blue. This process usually gives the best results. Invariably the moment of realization must have been preceded by a period of preparation. In origami terms, working with a few selected techniques gives familiarity and can trigger a spontaneous creative surge. Models suggested this way need only a little extra work to complete.

Creativity in practice

Which path to follow?

There is no single way to create. Creation is an imprecise art. Usually several of the processes outlined above are employed together in the creation of a single model. The path to follow is the one (or ones) which suit you best. The important thing is to keep trying, it does get easier with practice.

Other creative aides

Inspiration can be triggered in many ways. Adopting a favorite technique, perhaps, and developing a new model using that technique. Taking a new tack, i.e. tackling a subject nobody has yet done, or tackling an old subject from a fresh viewpoint. Brainstorming as a technique can open up new viewpoint ideas. Be open to sources outside origami and be prepared to adapt them. Set a new target — fold a recognizable model in only five steps, for example. Perhaps you might consider a change of philosophy — start with a triangular paper, or allow more than one piece in the finished model. Dare to do something different.

When creating a complex model, try splitting the model into smaller parts and work on each part separately. The separate papers can be fixed together later and any anomalies worked out.

Don't let yourself be sidetracked. Ignore all the exciting distractions of which paper to choose, what color to fold with, etc. Do it the hard way: use brown wrapping paper (if it's an animal, say) or your most infrequently used colored paper (if you need color contrast). This way, you are more likely to make models that are independent of the paper used.

If you need a few incentives, then consider these. Creators get their work published in society publications (free books/magazines, free convention packs). Better creators get their work published for real (money, prestige, etc.) Go for it.

The creative cycle

The first step is learning basic techniques. In origami terms, this means folding everything and anything you can get hold of. The next step is usually improving existing models. The inspiration for this is in the form of "What if this model had a better property (shape, movement, etc.)?" The final step is producing your own complete models.

There is another "maturity" cycle which usually applies too, once some creative proficiency is achieved. Most creators discover that once they can improve on existing models then complex models are relatively easy to create. After a period of complex creations, realization dawns that, paradoxically, good simple models are even more difficult to create. Good simple models are rare. This is no coincidence.

Most creators go through creative highs and lows. During a high period models are tumble out at a faster rate than can be folded or diagramed. Inevitably, after a high there follows a low or fallow period when inspiration is lacking. The experience is (I imagine) similar to writer's block.

Goodness and badness

I define the term "good" as applied to an origami model as:
- instantly recognizable final model (strong outline)
- pleasing folding sequence
- economic use of paper
- easily obtainable starting paper size
- final model pleasing to the eye
- no design weaknesses (e.g. split back on animal).

The term "bad" as applied to an origami model is the opposite to "good", that is:
- poorly recognizable final model (weak outline)
- unpleasant folding sequence
- uneconomic use of paper
- awkward starting paper size
- ugly to look at
- design weaknesses are apparent.

There are good models in all classes, simple, intermediate and complex. One thought strikes me. More people are likely to fold a good simple model than a good intermediate or good complex model. Popularity is only one criteria of the success of a model. Critical acclaim is another. As in all artistic activities, there are no hard and fast rules; there are general guidelines perhaps or rules that only exist for breaking. Do your own thing.

Happy folding and creating!
David Petty

◆folds and bases ....

Before beginning the models, you should familiarise yourself with some of the basic folds. The main ones you will encounter are:

Valley fold

This is the basis for all origami models. For this you bring one edge of the paper up to meet the other — thus creating a "valley".

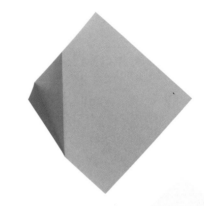

Mountain fold

This is the reverse of the valley fold. Here you fold one edge of the paper underneath the other — creating a "mountain."

There are also a number of bases and folds which form steps for many models. Steps for creating these are as follows:

Kite base

This is the easiest base, named after the shape it forms. Simply fold both edges of the sheet to meet the center line. Make sure both edges are lined up evenly before creasing firmly.

Squash

You will need to practice this, as it is very easy to wrinkle.

1 Take a 2x1 sheet folded in half to make a square of double thickness.

2 Take the edge of the paper to the crease, valley fold, and return.

3 Separate the layers and gently squash down on the top of the flap, flattening it evenly.

Petal fold

Begin with the squash fold.

1 Fold both corners of the squash to the center and return.

2 Mountain fold these corners inside. Lift the bottom point of the flap to meet the top. Make sure your creases are even, and firmly made.

Rabbit-ear fold

Commonly used to create ears, this fold makes a small moveable flap.

1 Fold the corners of the square to the center and return.

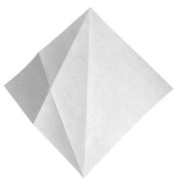

2 Fold the second corners of the square to the center and return.

3 Fold both corners of the square to the center.

4 The completed fold.

Inside reverse fold.

Reverse folds are where you reverse the direction of a previous crease.

1 Starting with a square with diagonal center fold, fold the tip at an angle. The point should lay outside the vertical edge.

2 Return the tip.

3 Open the layers and gently press the tip down. It is easy to crinkle this fold, so take care to only use the original creases.

4 To complete, bring the layers together again.

Outside reverse fold

Here the fold is outside the main part of the paper.

1 Begin with a square with a central diagonal fold. Fold the tip at an angle, with point laying outside the vertical edge.

2 Return the tip.

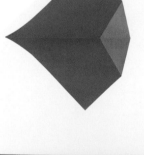

3 Open the layers and gently push the tip backwards. Use only existing creases.

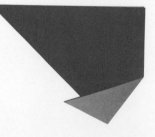

4 To complete, bring layers together again.

Inside crimp

Begin with a kite base, mountain-folded in half.

1 Choose an angle, then valley fold tip.

2 Now valley fold in the opposite direction.

3 Unfold. Refold using existing creases, with direction reversed.

4 Side view.

Outside crimp.

Begin in same way as inside crimp.

1 Valley fold tip to an angle.

2 Valley fold in the opposite direction. Unfold.

3 Now refold using existing creases, in the opposite direction.

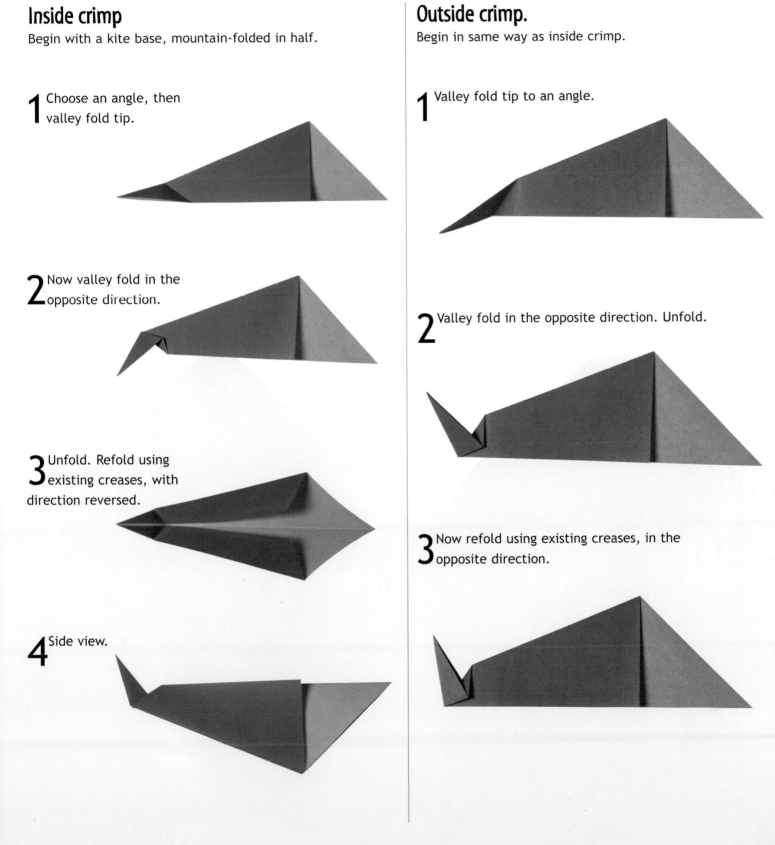

Waterbomb base

Start with a square, valley-folded from left to right.

1 Mountain fold top edge to bottom. Then valley fold diagonally top left corner to bottom right corner. Then diagonally valley fold top right to bottom left corner.

2 Push all creases into the center and gently flatten the paper as shown.

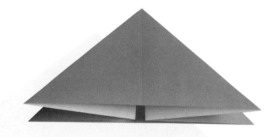

Squash fold

Here the fold is outside the main part of the paper.

1 Fold left edge to center and return.

2 Lift the flap upright, separate the layers and push down to flatten.

Blintz base

Start with square with two diagonal creases.

1 Valley fold each corner to the center point.

2 Fold creases firmly, ensuring edges stay even.

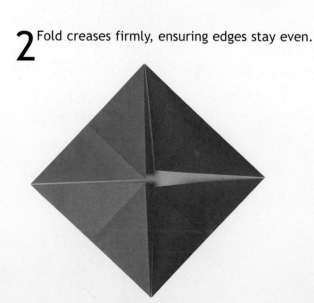

Fish base

Begin with a square, crease diagonally in half twice.

1 Create kite base.

2 Fold top tip down to meet the bottom tip. Mountain and valley fold as shown.

3 Lift the front flap along the crease.

4 Turn over for completed base.

Windmill base

Named for the shape it creates. Begin with a square sheet, creased in half both ways.

1 Valley fold top edge to center line. Repeat with bottom edge.

2 Fold both ends to center line.

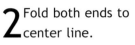

3 Pull out each corner in turn.

4 Thus creating four flaps.

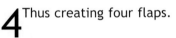

5 To complete, valley fold two of the flaps.

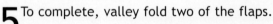

Preliminary base

Begin with a square sheet, creased diagonally.

1 Mountain fold top corner to bottom and return. Valley fold top left edge to bottom right edge. Valley fold top right edge to bottom left edge.

2 Bring all four corners together and carefully flatten along the crease.

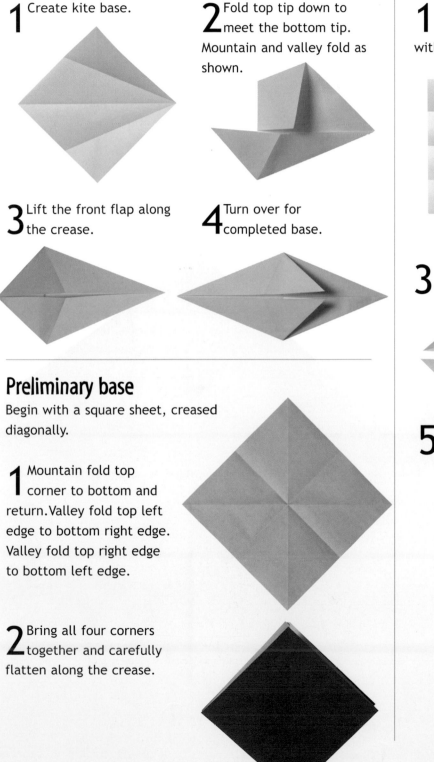

Bird base

This is a tricky base that begins with the preliminary base.

Stretched bird base

A variation on the previous bird base.

1 Valley fold left and right corners to center and return. Mountain fold top corner to the back and return.

2 Raise the bottom flap of the front layer and bring it to the top.

3 This is the result.

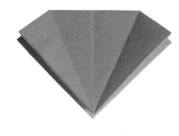

1 Begin with the standard bird base.

4 Turn over and fold the middle flap up.

5 Again lift the bottom flap of the front layer only and bring it to the top.

6 Fold down the top tips of both the top and bottom layers.

2 Turn over and rotate the base. Gently pull the inner flaps until the bottom point pops inside.

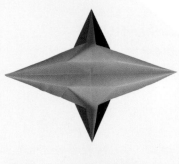

3 Flatten to complete.

7 The completed base.

Bird base

Fold a square in half both ways. Note that for this base the colored side of the paper is face up.

1 Fold all four corners to the center.

2 Form a preliminary base, with flaps face up.

3 On the top layer only, fold the sides to the center and return. Make sure that the closed end is at the top.

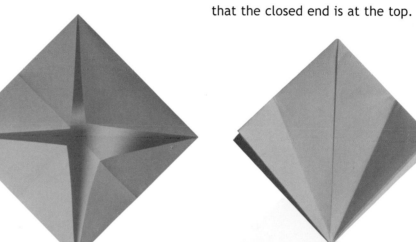

4 Petal fold front and back. Raise the upper layer and the sides will follow.

5 Pull out the hidden corners.

6 Fold the flaps down at both front and back.

7 Completed base.

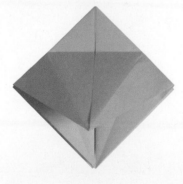

Sink fold

There are many valley and mountain folds in this, so make sure you are doing the right fold at the right time! Begin with a square, folded in half.

1 Form the waterbomb base with the color on the outside.

2 Fold front tip to the middle of the bottom edge, firmly crease, and return. Turn over and repeat. This clearly marks your creases.

3 Open out your sheet and check the creases.

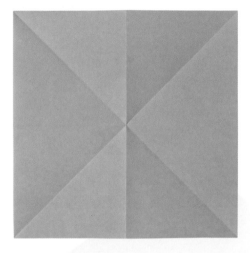

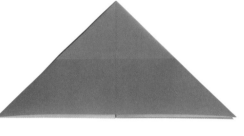

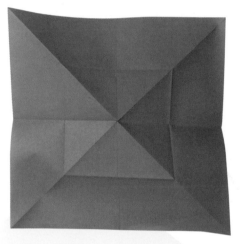

4 Now you need to put in a series of mountain folds, working round the sheet. First put in mountain folds in the outer corners, and then in the central square.

5 Push the sides towards the middle, at the same time as pushing down in the center.

6 Taking care to line up the folds exactly, continue bringing the corners together.

7 Completed.

Double sink fold

A variation on the previous fold – with double the number of folds used!

1 Form waterbomb base as before, with color on the outside.

2 Fold top tip to middle of bottom edge, crease and return. Repeat on the other side.

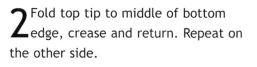

3 Fold the tip to this new crease, crease firmly and return. Repeat on other side.

4 Open out the sheet and again work round putting in mountain folds in the outer corners and inner square.

5 Push in from the sides, at the same time as pushing down in the center to bring the corners together.

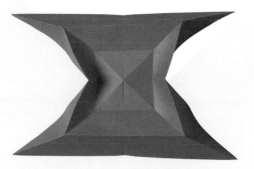

6 Partially open out to the single sink.

7 Push the center up to form the shape as shown.

8 Bring corners together — ensure you maintain the creases.

9 Completed.

Frog base

This is probably the most complicated of the bases and you will need a lot of practice!

1 Form the preliminary base.

2 Squash the right tip of the top layer.

3 Using existing creases, swing this flap to the other side.

4 Squash the left tip of the top layer in the same way.

5 Check all your creases are even and made firmly.

6 Turn over and squash right tip as before.

7 Swing this flap to the other side.

8 Squash left tip as before.

9 Valley fold the edges to the center and return. Make sure the creases go exactly to the point. Raise the top layer along a line that joins the folded edges, and petal fold.

10 Petal fold shown half way.

11 Repeat the petal fold on three more flaps to complete.

Portrait base ERIC KENNEWAY

This is another complicated base, which will require plenty of practice!

1 Precrease.

2 Precrease vertical, fold horizontal.

3 Inside reverse fold.

4 Precrease.

5 Squash.

6 Fold tip to point.

7 Fold edge to crease.

8 Swivel fold, pulling material from under triangle.

9 Fold flap back.

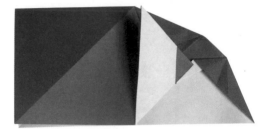

10 Rotate squash portion, turn over.

11 Repeat steps 7-9 on left-hand side.

12 Rotate squash portion.

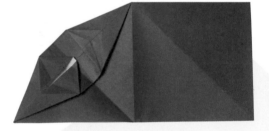

13 Squash.

14 Squash flap hidden inside to form nose.

Portrait base inverted

It is necessary to open the model to swing the front flap over and behind.

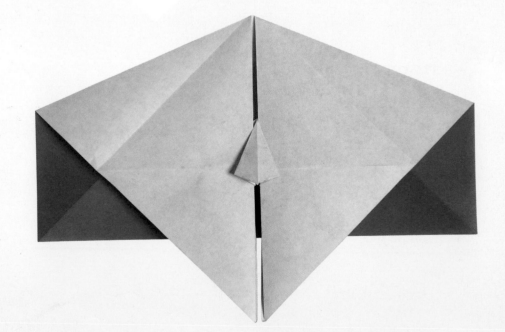

1 simple models

Not too taxing on time or energy, these are simple to fold but still rewarding. Beginners start here.

goldfish

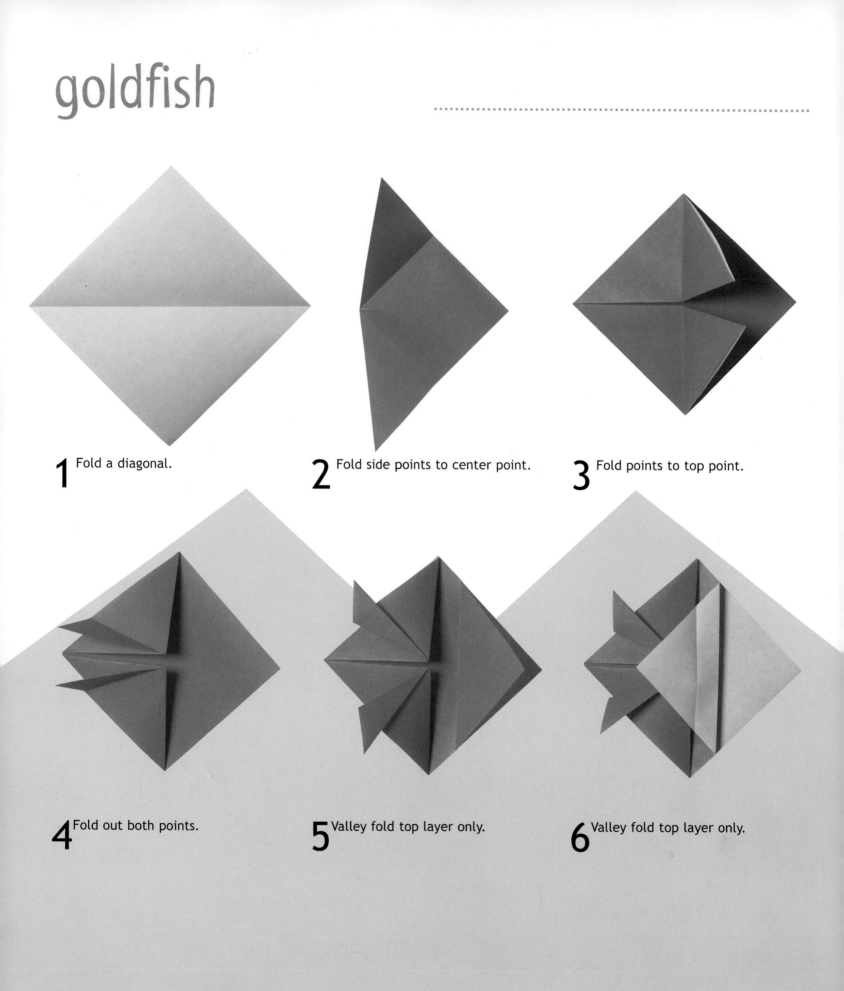

1 Fold a diagonal.

2 Fold side points to center point.

3 Fold points to top point.

4 Fold out both points.

5 Valley fold top layer only.

6 Valley fold top layer only.

◆ 24

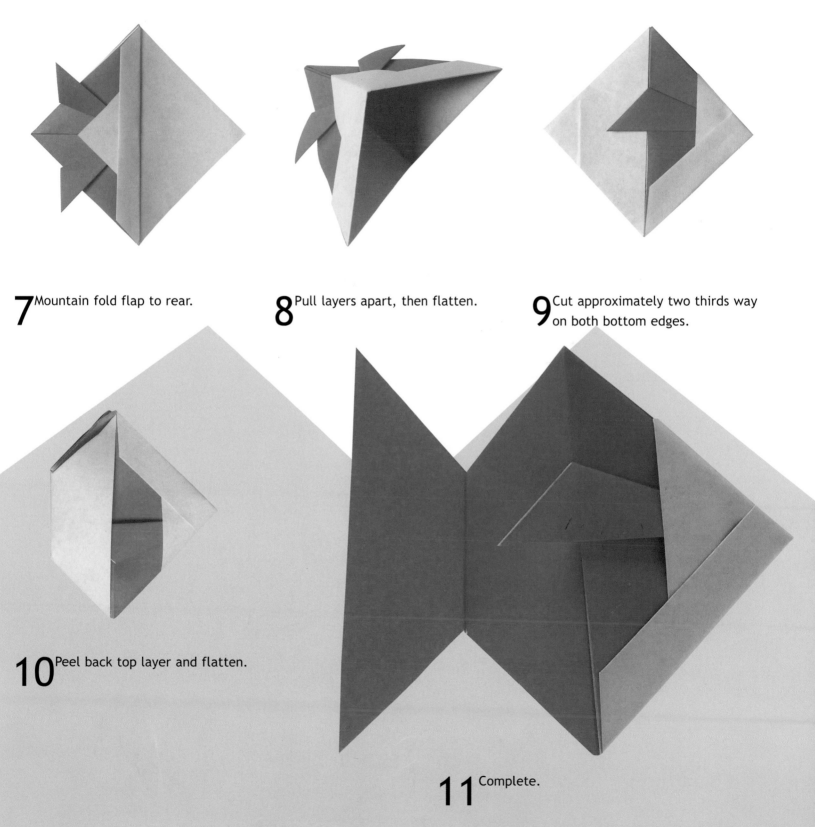

7 Mountain fold flap to rear.

8 Pull layers apart, then flatten.

9 Cut approximately two thirds way on both bottom edges.

10 Peel back top layer and flatten.

11 Complete.

lantern

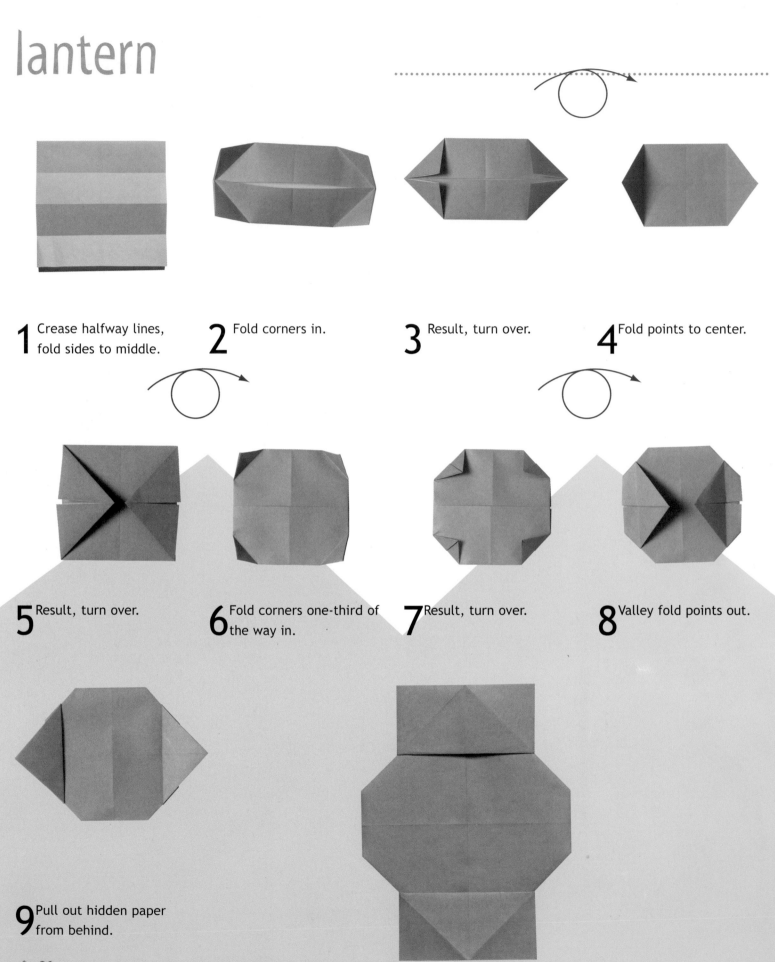

1 Crease halfway lines, fold sides to middle.

2 Fold corners in.

3 Result, turn over.

4 Fold points to center.

5 Result, turn over.

6 Fold corners one-third of the way in.

7 Result, turn over.

8 Valley fold points out.

9 Pull out hidden paper from behind.

church

1 Form waterbomb base.

2 Valley fold points to top point.

3 Mountain fold points to top point and repeat at back.

4 Squash front flaps.

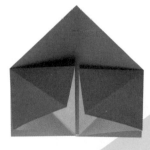

5 Squash rear flaps.

6 Mountain fold sides behind center.

7 Lift front layer and squash.

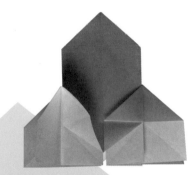

8 Repeat squashes at rear.

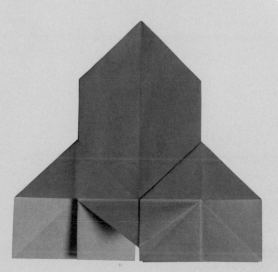

9 Fold up flap, repeat at rear.

10 Complete.

buffet server

1 Fold in half.

2 Fold in half, rotate so 4 corners are at the top.

3 Fold top layer down.

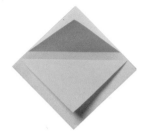

4 Fold top layer down.

5 Fold top layer down.

6 Fold sides to rear — they will overlap.

7 Complete.

fluttering butterfly | folder

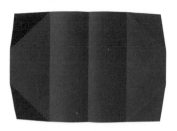

1 Crease both diagonals, leave one folded.

2 Fold folded edge over (approximately one third.)

1 Crease centerline fold corner to hit centerline. cut off above the meeting point
A-size sheet: start at step 2
Square sheet: start step 1

2 Fold sides to center and return. Fold corners to new creases. Fold sides to center again

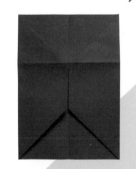

3 Valley fold in half.

4 Fold wings down at right angles from point at which front edge of wing meets diagonal.

3 Fold top part behind turn over.

4 Fold bottom part up (crease lies at top of 45° edges behind) and tuck into top pockets.

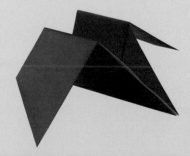

5 Launch as an aeroplane model and it will spin to the ground.

5 Valley fold in half.

6 Two pockets. One big or four small pockets inside.

miter

Use newspaper to make a wearable hat.

1 Crease lengthways, fold short edges together.

2 Fold double thickness.

3 Result, turn over.

4 Fold to centerline.

5 Fold top layer up.

6 Fold points behind, fold bottom layer behind.

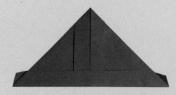

7 Fold points between layers.

8 Fold points under central strips.

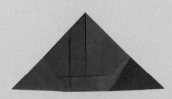

sailboat 1

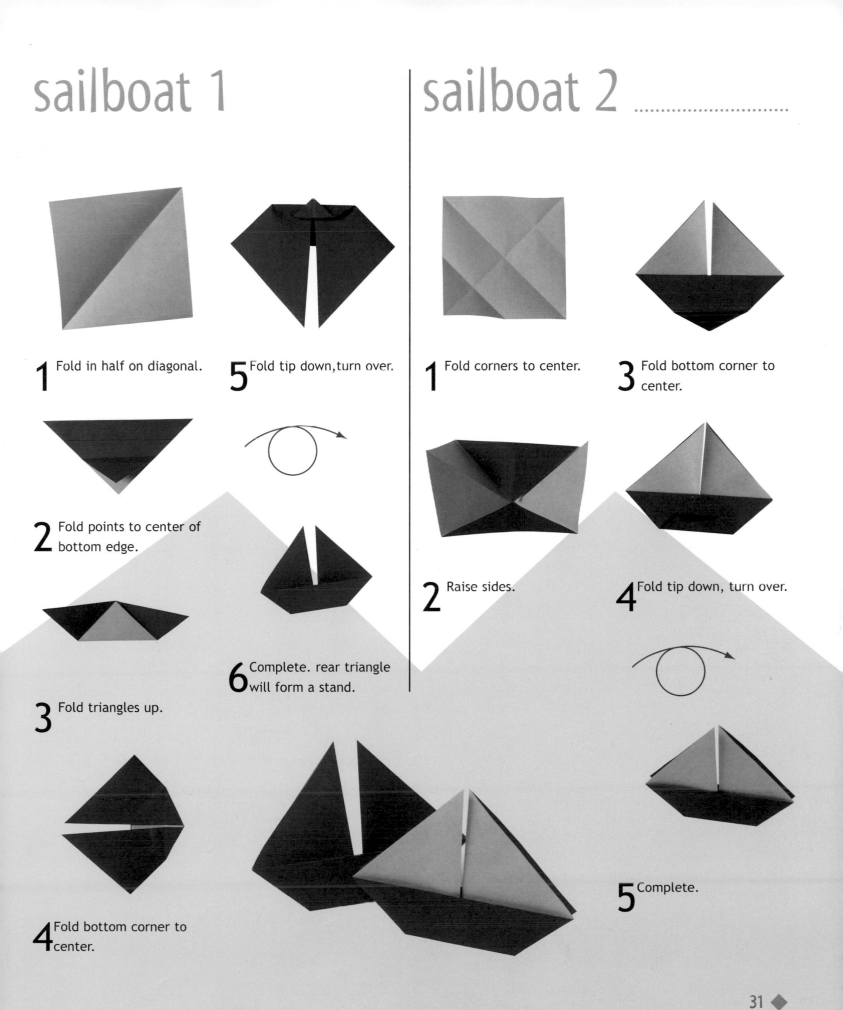

1 Fold in half on diagonal.

2 Fold points to center of bottom edge.

3 Fold triangles up.

4 Fold bottom corner to center.

5 Fold tip down, turn over.

6 Complete. rear triangle will form a stand.

sailboat 2

1 Fold corners to center.

2 Raise sides.

3 Fold bottom corner to center.

4 Fold tip down, turn over.

5 Complete.

cowboy hat

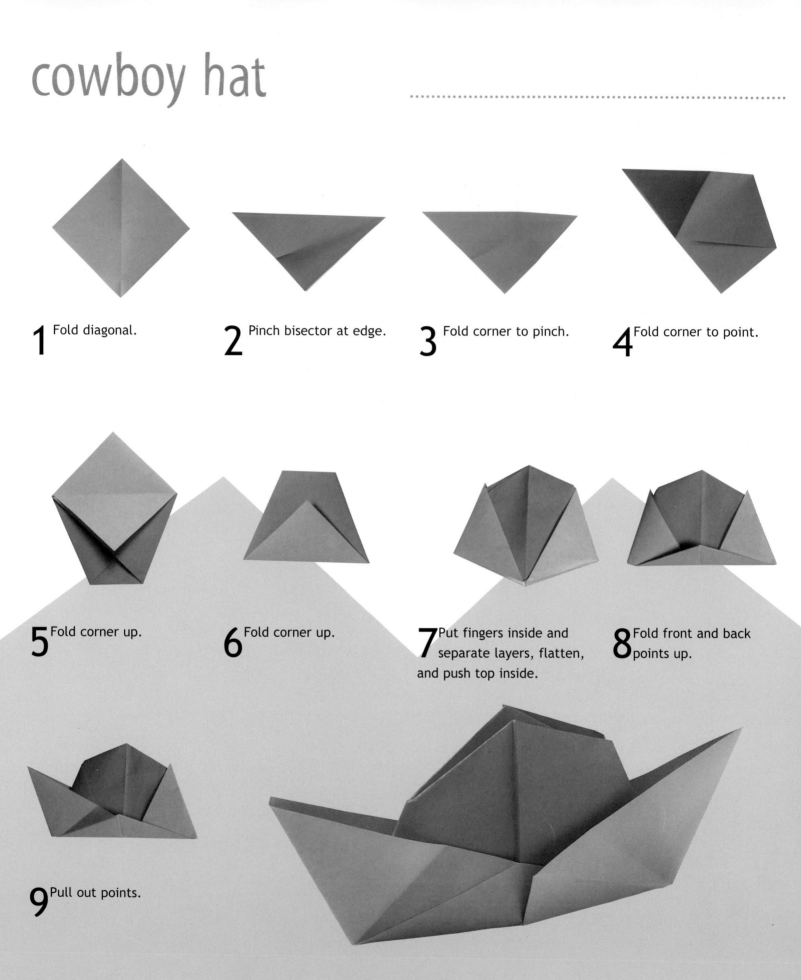

1 Fold diagonal.

2 Pinch bisector at edge.

3 Fold corner to pinch.

4 Fold corner to point.

5 Fold corner up.

6 Fold corner up.

7 Put fingers inside and separate layers, flatten, and push top inside.

8 Fold front and back points up.

9 Pull out points.

snapper

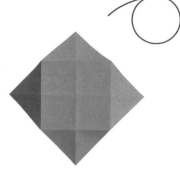  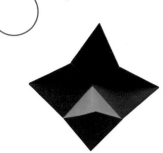 

1 Fold corners to center, turn over.

2 Fold corners to center, turn over.

3 Form waterbomb base, lifting top flap.

4 To make snap, hold either side of head, push hands together, then return.

star box

  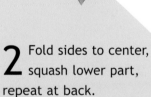 

1 Form preliminary base.

2 Fold sides to center, squash lower part, repeat at back.

3 Bookfold front and back.

4 Fold sides to center, repeat at back.

 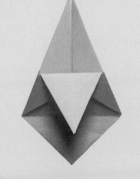 

5 Fold and return lower triangle.

6 Fold point down, repeat on all four sides.

7 Insert finger to form box.

four point star

Two squares are required, folding is different for each.

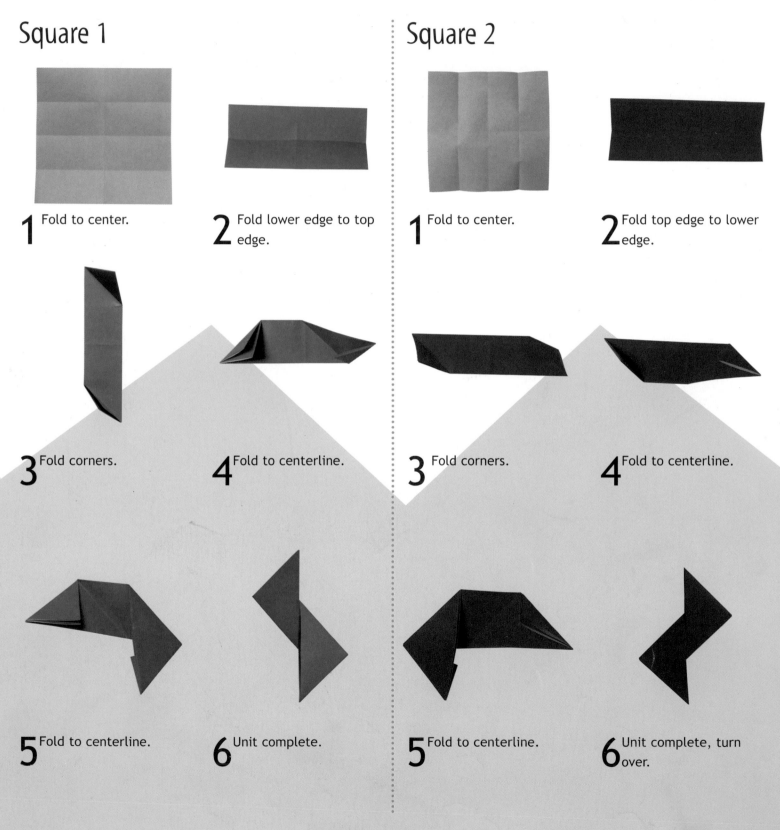

Square 1

1 Fold to center.

2 Fold lower edge to top edge.

3 Fold corners.

4 Fold to centerline.

5 Fold to centerline.

6 Unit complete.

Square 2

1 Fold to center.

2 Fold top edge to lower edge.

3 Fold corners.

4 Fold to centerline.

5 Fold to centerline.

6 Unit complete, turn over.

Assembly

A Tuck points inside pockets.

B Result, turn over.

C Tuck points inside pockets.

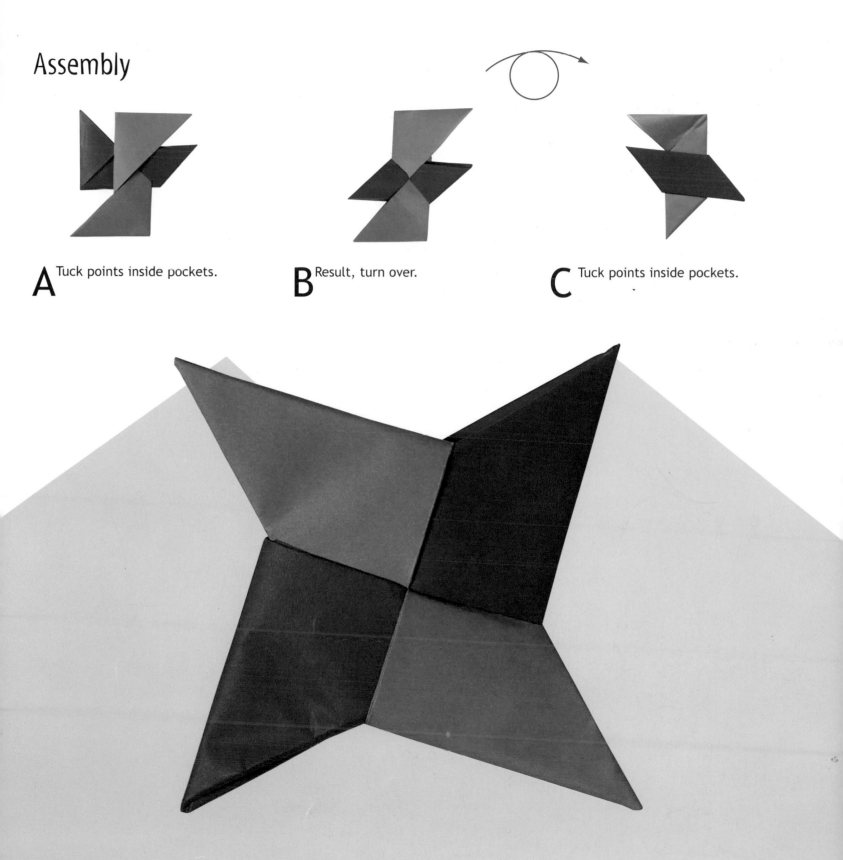

seed packet

Fold with any rectangle.

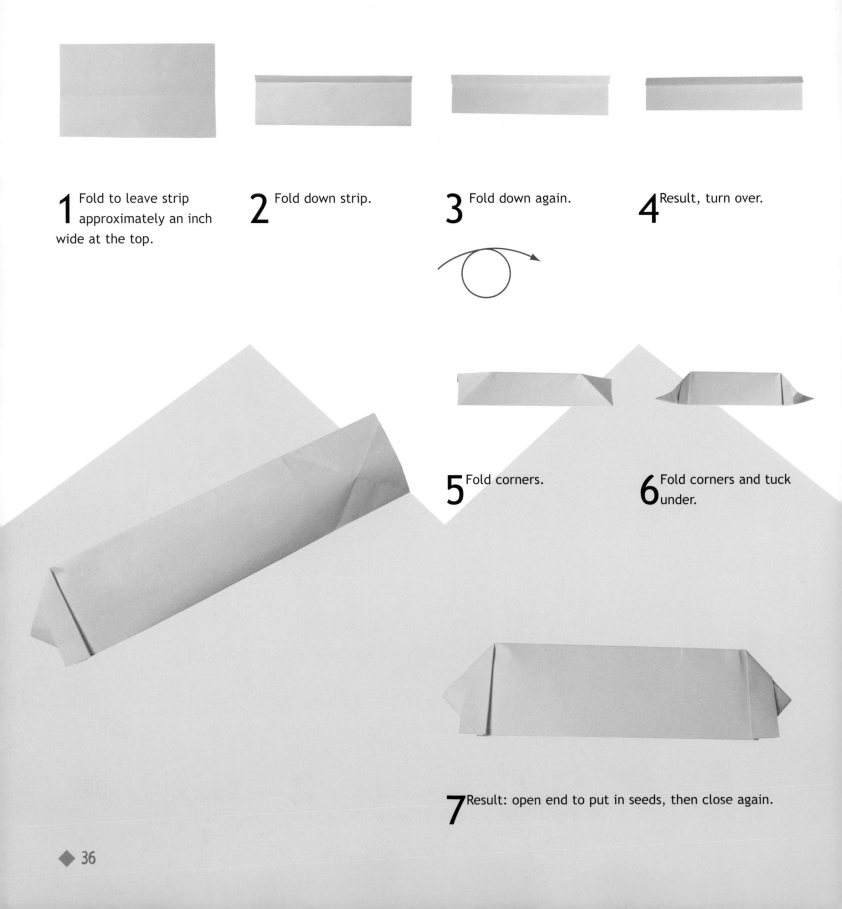

1 Fold to leave strip approximately an inch wide at the top.

2 Fold down strip.

3 Fold down again.

4 Result, turn over.

5 Fold corners.

6 Fold corners and tuck under.

7 Result: open end to put in seeds, then close again.

candle

(David Petty)

1 Fold one corner to center.

2 Fold sides of triangle under and top edges down.

3 Result, turn over.

4 Fold corners to center.

5 Fold flap down, allow point at back to flip.

6 Fold sides in, tuck one inside the other.

7 Fold up bottom triangle, turn over.

composite doll

(David Petty)

Head

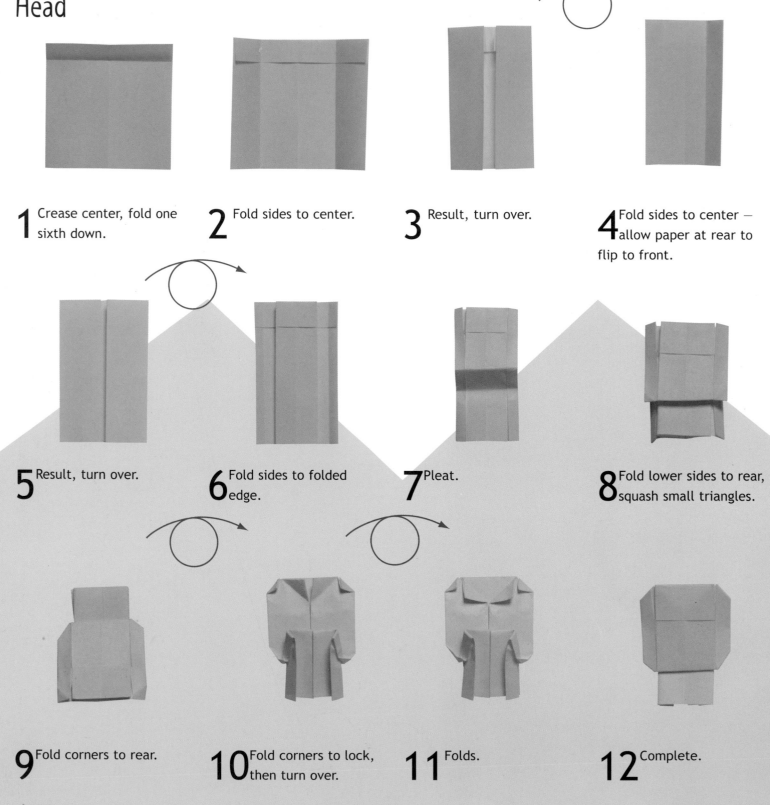

1 Crease center, fold one sixth down.

2 Fold sides to center.

3 Result, turn over.

4 Fold sides to center — allow paper at rear to flip to front.

5 Result, turn over.

6 Fold sides to folded edge.

7 Pleat.

8 Fold lower sides to rear, squash small triangles.

9 Fold corners to rear.

10 Fold corners to lock, then turn over.

11 Folds.

12 Complete.

Lower part

1 Pleat central eighths.

2 Mountain fold in half.

3 Pull top layers sideways, flatten at top.

4 Result, turn over.

5 Fold flap up.

6 Fold sides in, squash at sides.

7 Result, turn over.

8 Complete.

Upper part

As lower body to step 5, then . . .

6a Fold sides to center, squash at top.

7a Result, turn over.

8a Complete.

Assembly insert rear flaps into pockets.

Longer skirt as lower body to step 2.

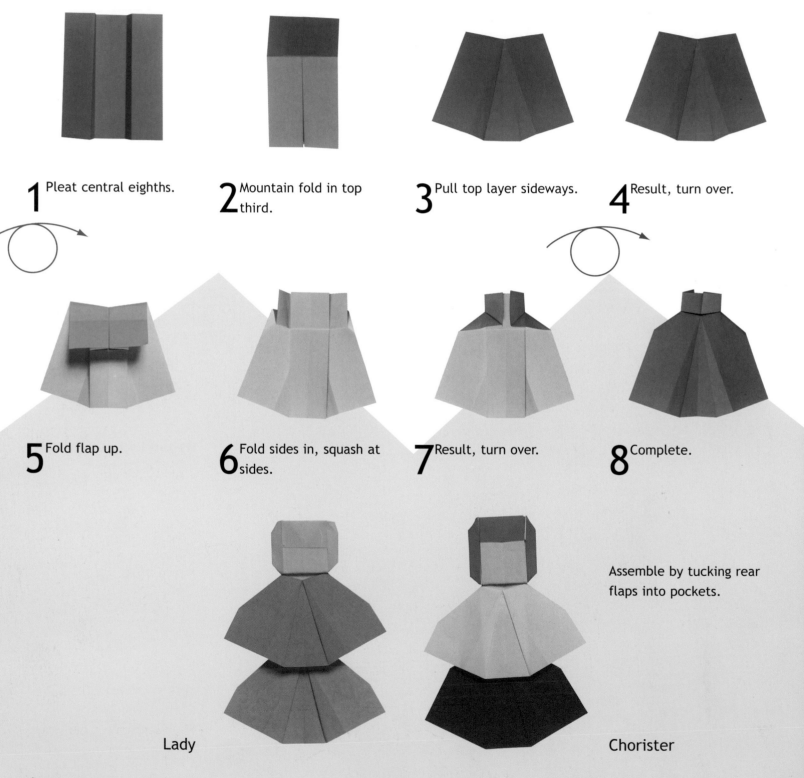

1 Pleat central eighths.

2 Mountain fold in top third.

3 Pull top layer sideways.

4 Result, turn over.

5 Fold flap up.

6 Fold sides in, squash at sides.

7 Result, turn over.

8 Complete.

Assemble by tucking rear flaps into pockets.

Lady

Chorister

drinking cup ring

(David Petty)

2 ³/₄-in. start paper gives 5¹/₂-in. diameter ring D; 4-in. paper makes ring E.

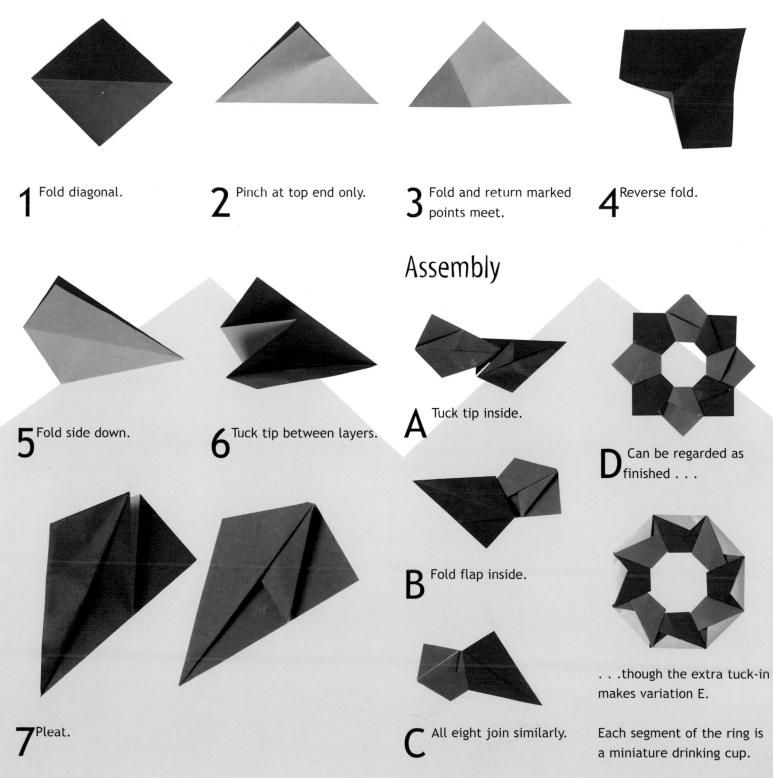

1 Fold diagonal.

2 Pinch at top end only.

3 Fold and return marked points meet.

4 Reverse fold.

Assembly

5 Fold side down.

6 Tuck tip between layers.

A Tuck tip inside.

B Fold flap inside.

7 Pleat.

C All eight join similarly.

D Can be regarded as finished . . .

. . .though the extra tuck-in makes variation E.

Each segment of the ring is a miniature drinking cup.

flapping bird

(David Petty)

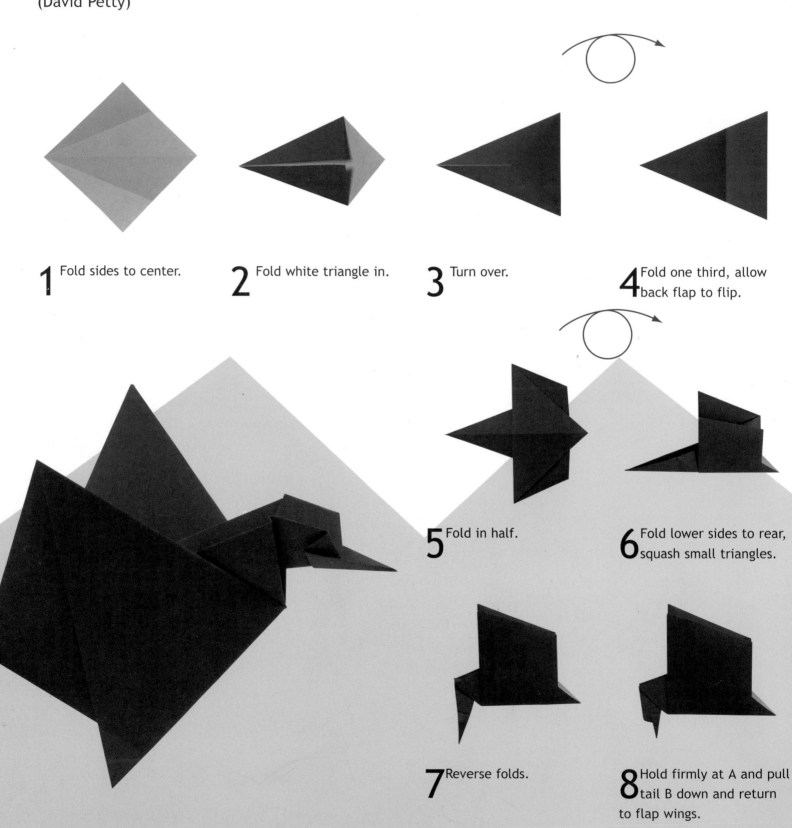

1 Fold sides to center.

2 Fold white triangle in.

3 Turn over.

4 Fold one third, allow back flap to flip.

5 Fold in half.

6 Fold lower sides to rear, squash small triangles.

7 Reverse folds.

8 Hold firmly at A and pull tail B down and return to flap wings.

flight of fancy

(David Petty)

This model will make with 16, 17 or 18 units. It is best with an even number to preserve symmetry.

Assembly

1 Crease diagonal, fold sides to it.

2 Result, turn over.

A Insert flaps at rear of one unit into pockets at front of another.

3 Marked points meet; fold only on side opposite marked point.

4 Reverse fold.

5 Make 16, the geometrically perfect number. The ring may also be formed with a couple of additional units, then closed and flattened.

B The back of the darker unit lines up with the pocket lining — there is no gap here. The tip of the beak touches top edge of flap fold at right angles Marked points meet. Tuck tip inside

C Two units joined. Tip of beak touches top edge of flap. Assemble all units similarly.

Front (flight)

Back (fancy)

green cross

(David Petty)

Model based on the British Pharmacy logo.

Assembly

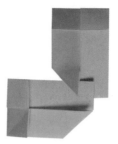

1 Fold left edge to center front, right edge to center behind.

2 Fold to centerline and return.

A Slide white corner into pocket.

B Fold inside corner using bisector from step 3.

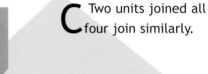

C Two units joined all four join similarly.

3 Fold and return angle bisector, then inside reverse on crease made in step 2.

4 Fold edge behind, reverse fold at corner.

5 Unit complete, make four.

happicoat

(Traditional)

1 Crease centerlines, fold top edge to lower edge.

2 Fold and return.

3 Fold to crease.

4 Fold top layer only.

5 Result, turn over and rotate.

6 Fold down.

7 Fold to centerline.

8 Result, turn over.

9 Raise lower layer and pull side flaps out.

10 Result, turn over.

11 Complete.

heart page marker

1 Fold and return.

2 Fold lower corners to center.

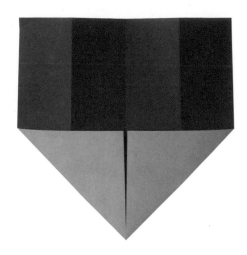

3 Fold to centerline, top part only.

4 Fold and return, between vertical creases, halfway to white edge.

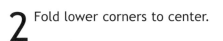

5 Fold and return, between vertical creases, halfway to crease in step 4.

6 Fold and return to form cross between vertical creases. Turn over.

◆ 46

7 Fold and return.

8 Collapse.

9 Fold edge down, squash corners.

10 Fold top corners in.

11 Raise lower flap and pull sides out, fold points in.

12 Fold corners inside.

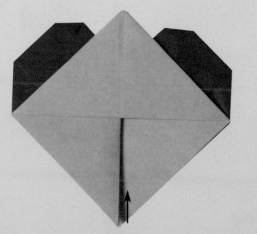

13 Page corner fits here turn over.

Finished heart on page.

flexagon

(Ibolya Tuzy)

Flexagons are special structures that change shape when manipulated.

Use same size square for all pieces. It is best to use thicker paper to avoid paper tearing.

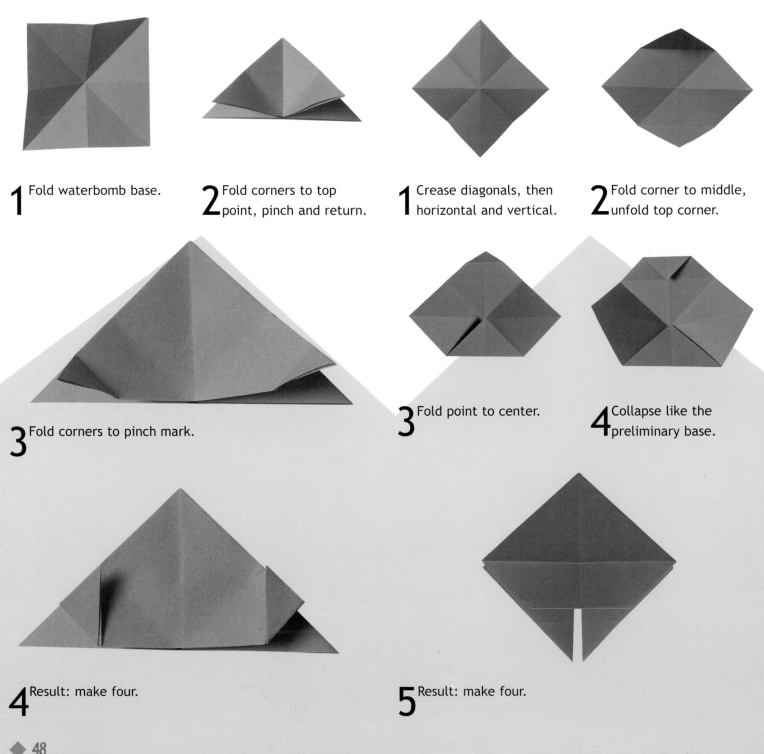

Part 1

1 Fold waterbomb base.

2 Fold corners to top point, pinch and return.

3 Fold corners to pinch mark.

4 Result: make four.

Part 2

1 Crease diagonals, then horizontal and vertical.

2 Fold corner to middle, unfold top corner.

3 Fold point to center.

4 Collapse like the preliminary base.

5 Result: make four.

Assembly

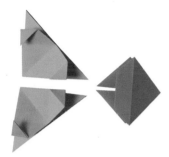   

A Insert flaps of first unit into pockets in second unit.
Ensure it is the correct way round so that small triangular flaps go under front pocket.
Large flaps in rear pocket.

B Now fold flap into pocket, behind triangular flaps.

C Result, units are locked. Add remaining units in the same way

D Model complete.

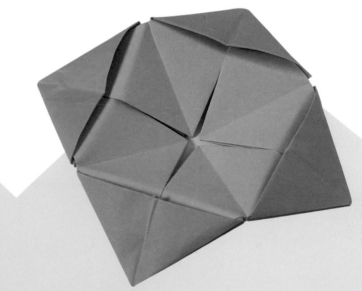

START THE ACTION SEQUENCE BY folding corners behind to get a flat square....

fold to get a preliminary base...

rotate out the points....

to get a salt cellar, continue rotating...

continue rotating...

to form a star-shape, continue rotating.....

to get a table, continue to return to flat square...

MANIPULATE YOUR FLEXAGON THROUGH ALL ITS SHAPES A COUPLE OF TIMES UNTIL IT BECOMES SUPPLE. YOU CAN THEN TRY GOING BACKWARDS THROUGH THE SEQUENCE.

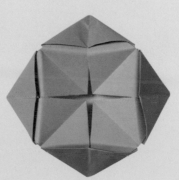

fancy basket

(Traditional)

1 Crease both diagonals.

2 Crease horizontal and vertical.

3 Fold edges to center and return.

4 Fold corners to center at back and return.

 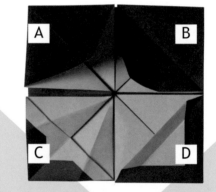 

5 Fold centers of edges to center.

6 Follow sequence A-B-C-D on all corners.

7 Result. Fold a second paper, same size as first, but omit step 6d.

 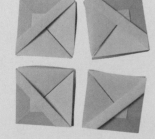  

8 Cut the second sheet.

Shows result.

9 Follow the sequence a-b as shown for each part of the second sheet.

10 Final composite, turn over.

handle

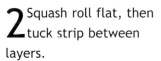

11 Push in the sides.

12 To 3D the model, turn over — mountain folds at corners are hard folds — these can be soft folds.

1 Roll a same size paper to form a handle.

2 Squash roll flat, then tuck strip between layers.

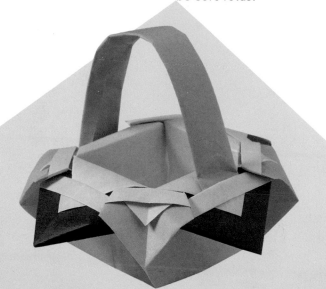

square coaster

(David Petty)

Assembly

1 Fold diagonal.

2 Fold corner to point and return.

A Tuck point into pocket.

B Fold small triangle inside, and large over it.

 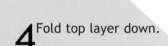 

3 Inside reverse.

4 Fold top layer down.

C Completed join. Add remaining units similarly.

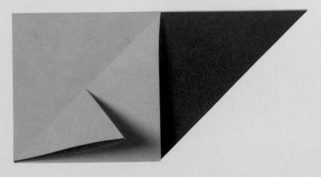  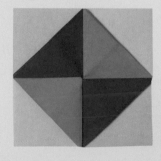

5 Fold along folded edge and return. Make four units.

Back.

Front.

intermediate models

These take more time and some understanding, and are for those beyond the basics.

kettle

(Traditional)

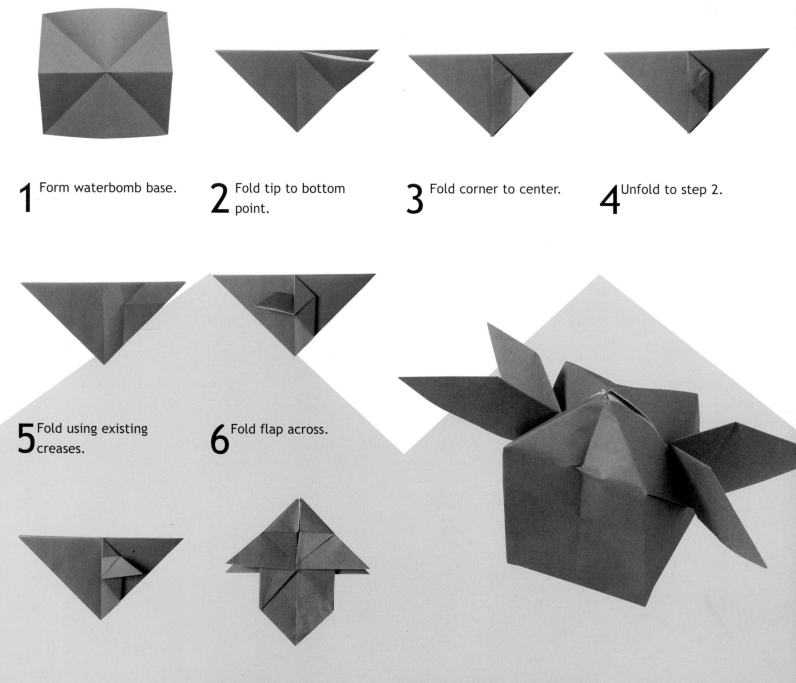

1 Form waterbomb base.

2 Fold tip to bottom point.

3 Fold corner to center.

4 Unfold to step 2.

5 Fold using existing creases.

6 Fold flap across.

8 Result; inflate to 3D model.

This will operate as a kettle, using a candle as heater BUT ONLY under adult supervision!

egg-laying hen

(Traditional)

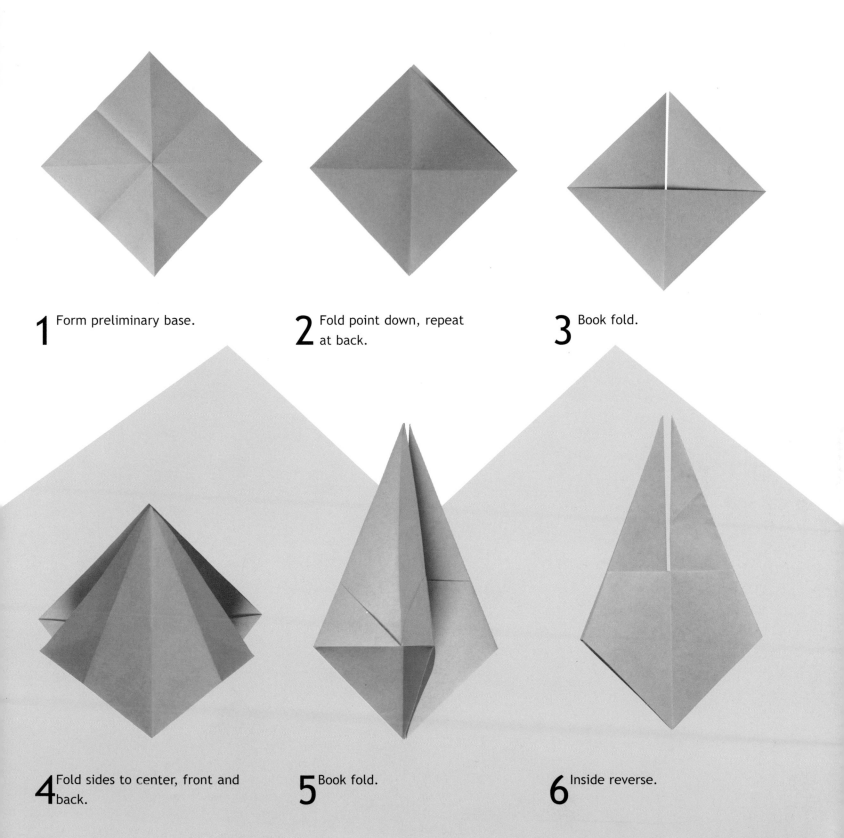

1 Form preliminary base.

2 Fold point down, repeat at back.

3 Book fold.

4 Fold sides to center, front and back.

5 Book fold.

6 Inside reverse.

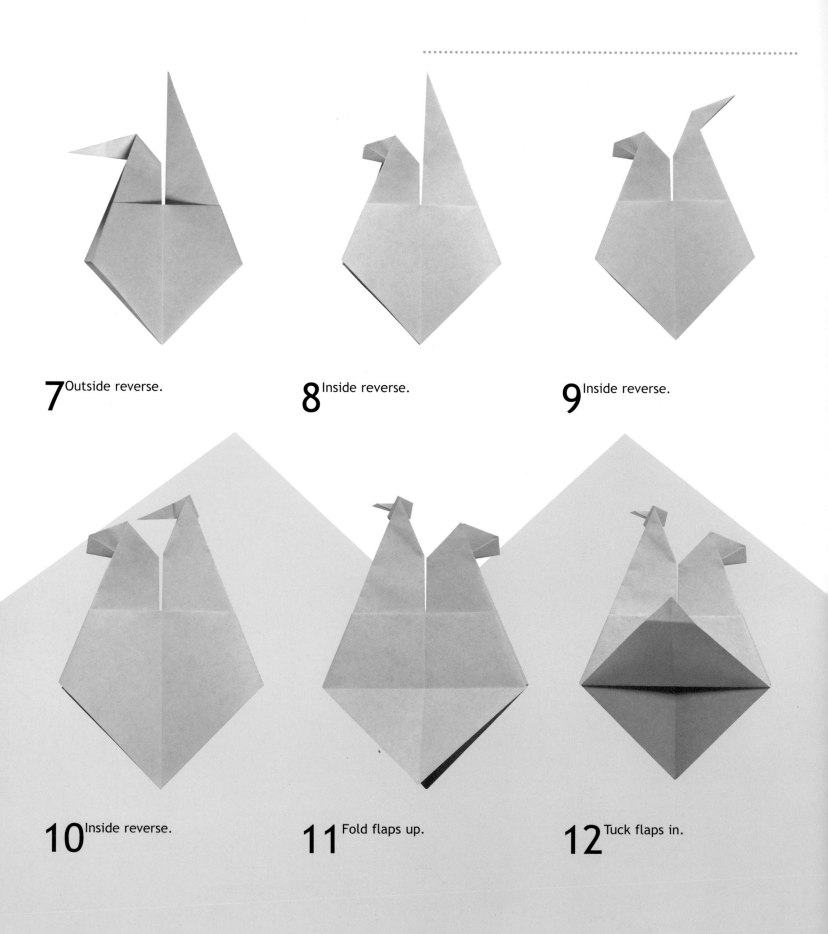

7 Outside reverse.

8 Inside reverse.

9 Inside reverse.

10 Inside reverse.

11 Fold flaps up.

12 Tuck flaps in.

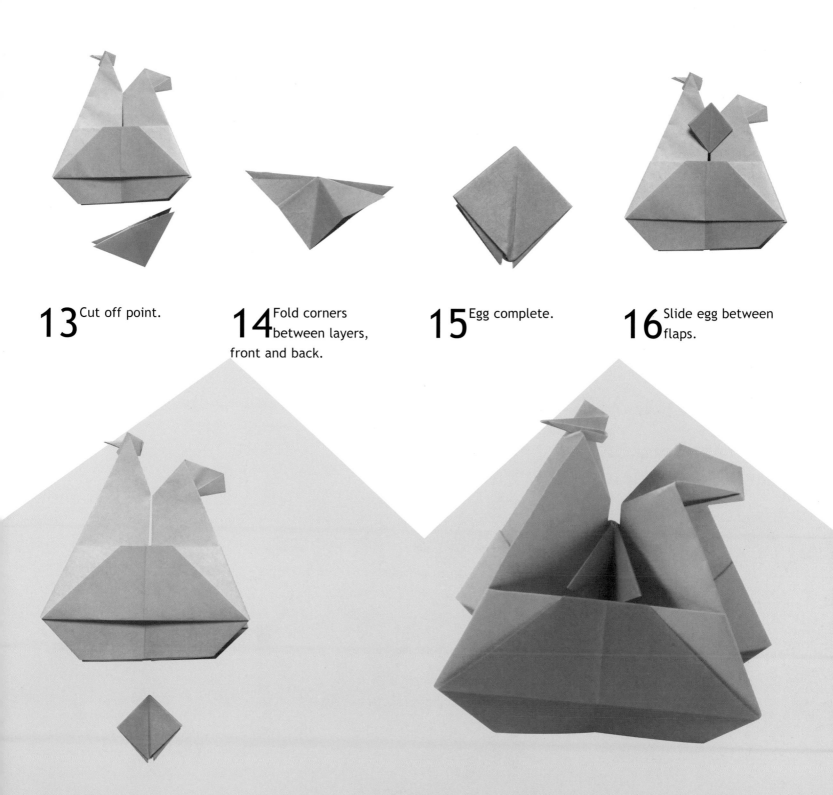

13 Cut off point.

14 Fold corners between layers, front and back.

15 Egg complete.

16 Slide egg between flaps.

17 Egg emerges.

Work head and tail up and down.

star

(Traditional)

MAKING AN EQUILATERAL TRIANGLE FROM A RECTANGLE.

Newspaper can be used.

  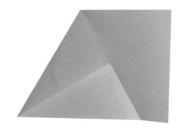 

1 Crease in center.

2 Fold corner to crease, fold starts at bottom corner.

3 Fold along edge of folded triangle.

4 Tuck triangle inside equilateral triangle complete turn over to plain side to make star.

MAKING THE STAR

Start with side without edges on top.

  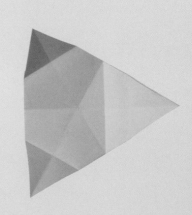

1 Crease centerlines.

2 Take each point to center and return.

3 Take point to center of opposite side.

 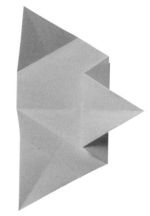 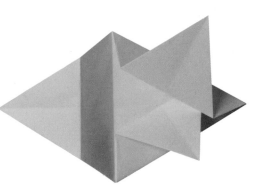

4 Fold out point on existing crease.

5 Repeat steps 3 and 4 on next point.

6 Repeat steps 3 and 4 on the next point.

7 Bring layer underneath to front.

pagoda

(Traditional)

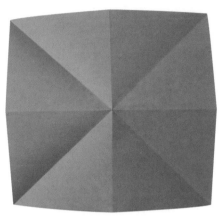

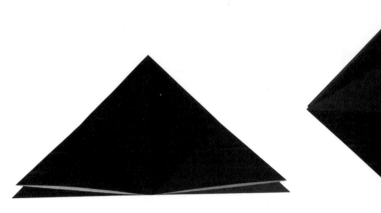

1 Form waterbomb base.

2 Fold corners to top point. Repeat at back.

3 Fold corners to bottom point and return, Repeat at back.

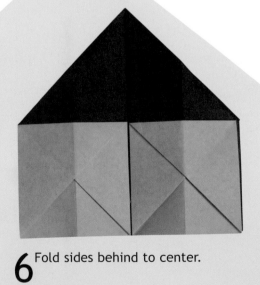

4 Open each flap and squash.

5 Fold top layer only.

6 Fold sides behind to center.

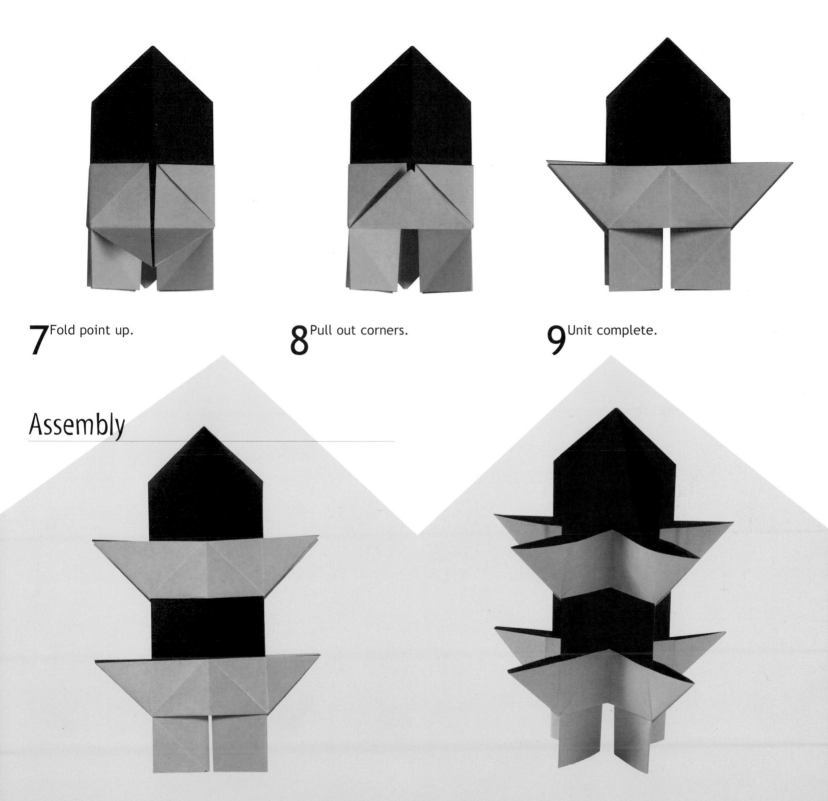

7 Fold point up.

8 Pull out corners.

9 Unit complete.

Assembly

A Slide top unit onto lower unit, and tuck the flaps into the pockets of the lower unit.

For best effect, fold units from successively reduced size paper e.g. 5"-4³/₄"-4¹/₂"-4¹/₄"- 4"-3³/₄"-3¹/₂"-3¹/₄"-3".

lighthouse bookmark

(Traditional)

1 Fold diagonals, then horizontal crease, and finally collapse into waterbomb base.

2 Fold points to top point.

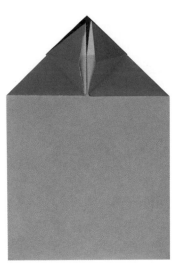

3 Squash both flaps.

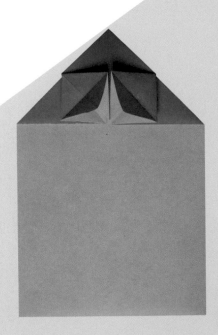

4 Fold top triangle, both sides.

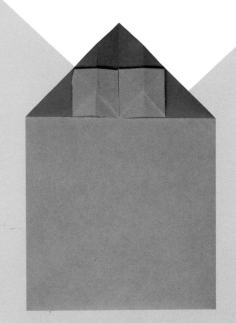

5 Fold edges back to center.

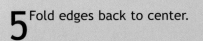

6 Fold triangle up.

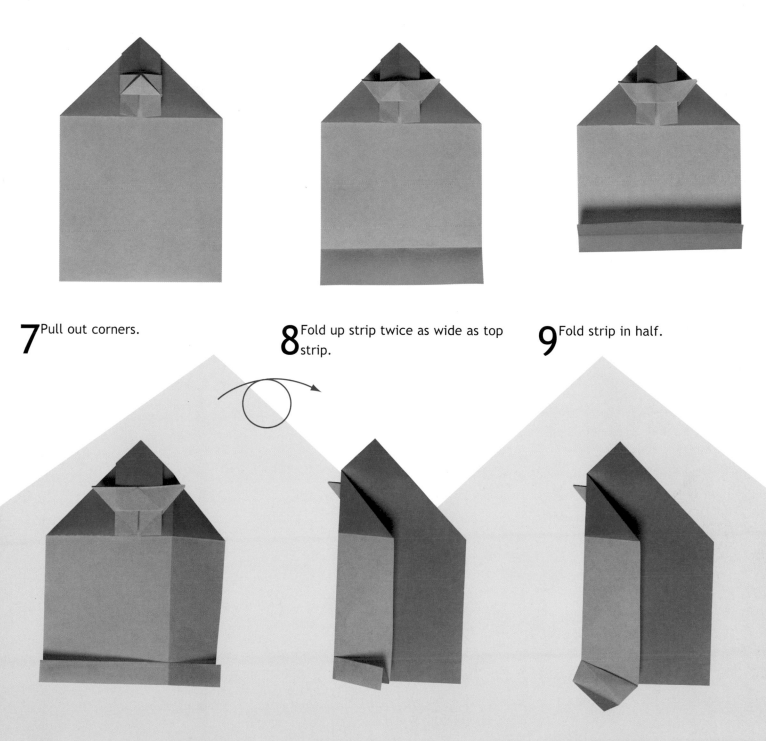

7 Pull out corners.

8 Fold up strip twice as wide as top strip.

9 Fold strip in half.

10 Fold edge to back, fold passes approximately halfway along top white triangle. Turn model over.

11 Pull down concertina edge and flatten.

12 Fold edge to line up with colored edge.

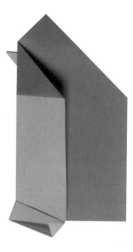

13 Fold edge to line up with colored edge.

14 Fold edge to line up with colored edge and repeat in mirror image steps 11,12,13. Finally, tuck right flap into left flap white triangle to lock.

15 Result. Turn over.

persimmon

(Traditional)

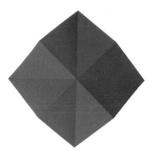 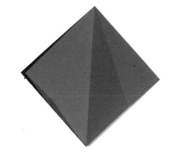  

1 Form preliminary base.

2 Fold and return, repeat at back.

3 Squash, repeat on all four flaps.

4 Bookfold front and back.

5 Fold down point.

6 Fold corners behind - repeat steps 5 & 6 on remaining points.

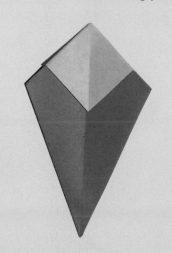

7 Inflate.

carrier pigeon

(Traditional)

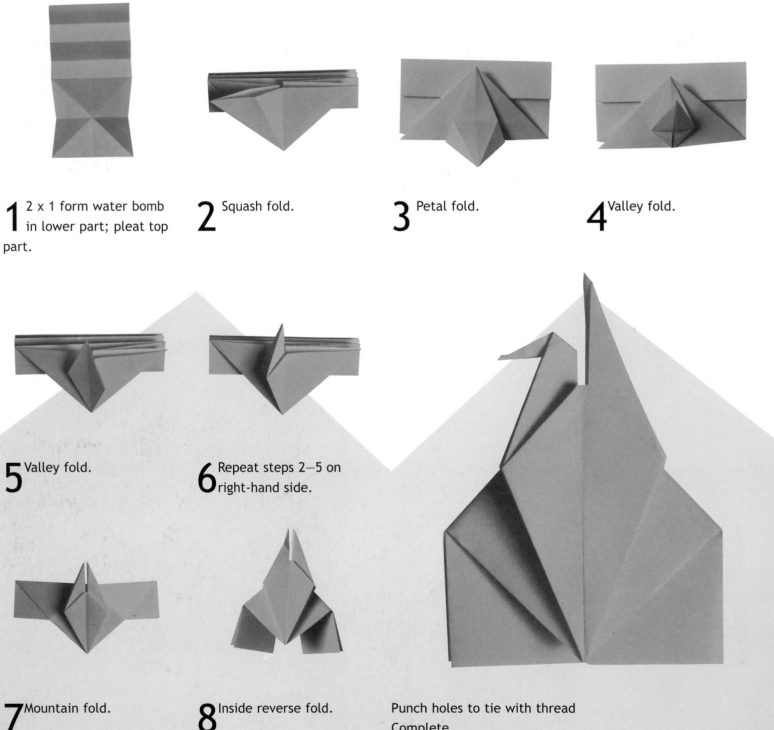

1 2 x 1 form water bomb in lower part; pleat top part.

2 Squash fold.

3 Petal fold.

4 Valley fold.

5 Valley fold.

6 Repeat steps 2—5 on right-hand side.

7 Mountain fold.

8 Inside reverse fold.

Punch holes to tie with thread Complete.

fancy box

(Traditional)

1 Precrease diagonals then blintz.

2 Result; turn over.

3 Blintz again.

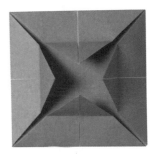

4 Fold corners to outer edge.

5 Result; turn over.

6 Pleat (sixths).

7 Press sides together at corners to form box.

8 Complete.

english policeman

(David Petty/Eric Kenneway)

Start — portrait base, inverted.

1 Raise back layer.

2 Fold top edges to centerline.

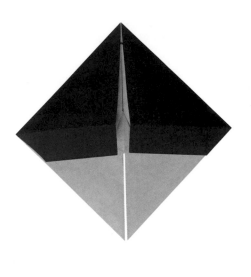

3 Fold flaps under.

4 Tuck flaps under nose.

5 Result; turn over.

6 These edges fold to touch the edges of the central flaps.

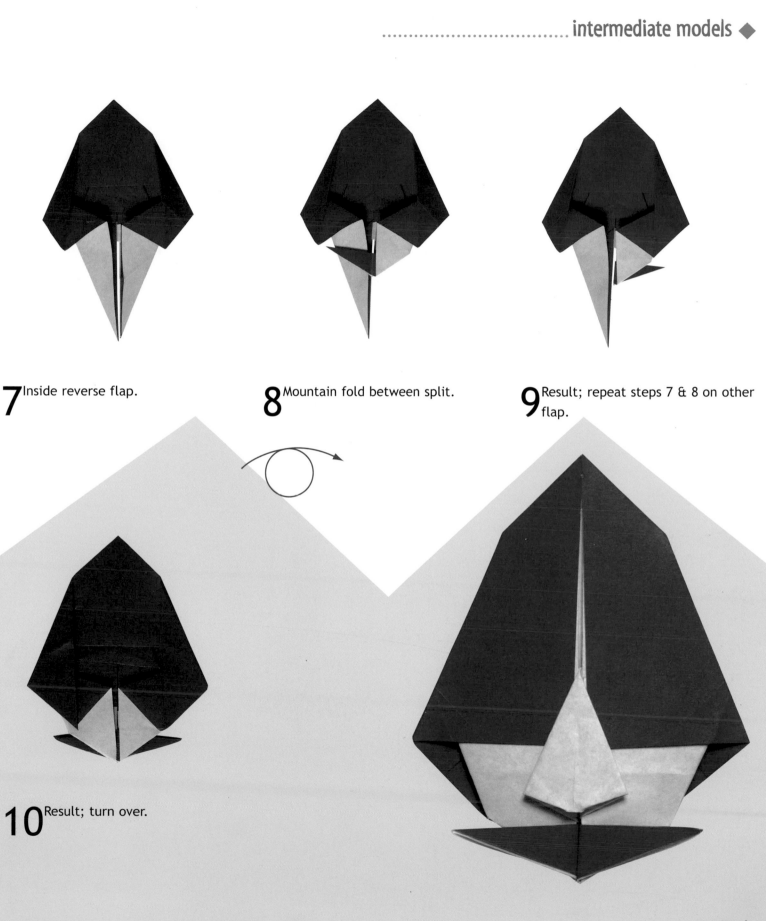

7 Inside reverse flap.

8 Mountain fold between split.

9 Result; repeat steps 7 & 8 on other flap.

10 Result; turn over.

page marker base

(David Petty)

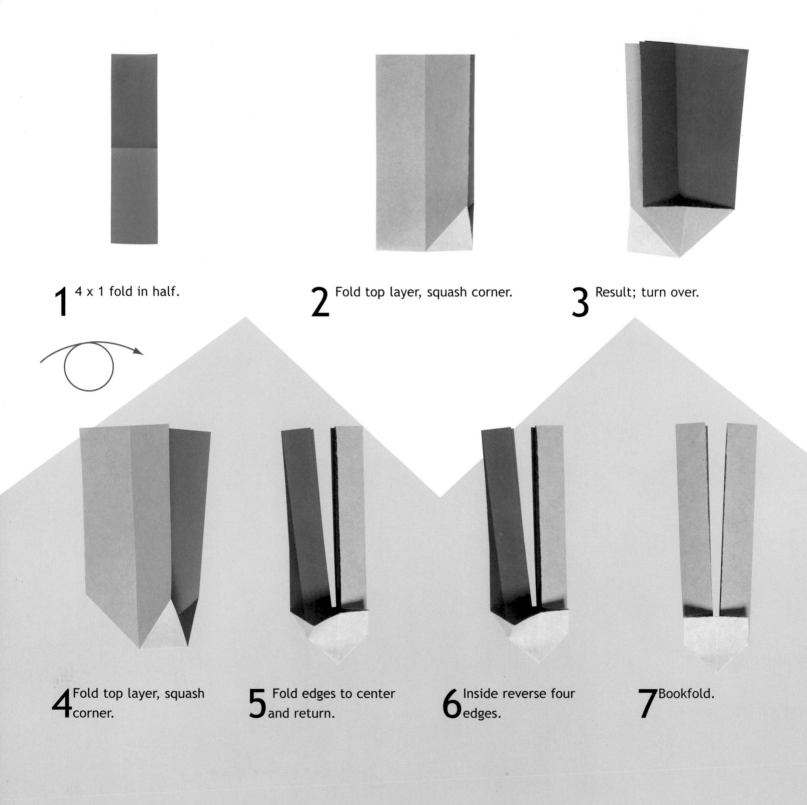

1 4 x 1 fold in half.

2 Fold top layer, squash corner.

3 Result; turn over.

4 Fold top layer, squash corner.

5 Fold edges to center and return.

6 Inside reverse four edges.

7 Bookfold.

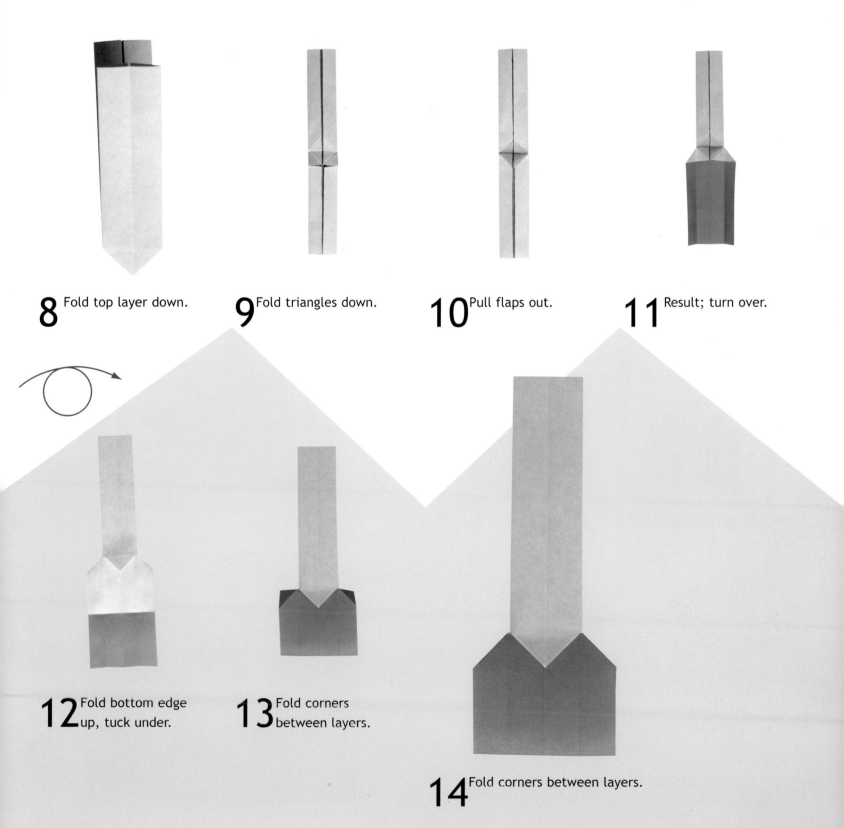

8 Fold top layer down.

9 Fold triangles down.

10 Pull flaps out.

11 Result; turn over.

12 Fold bottom edge up, tuck under.

13 Fold corners between layers.

14 Fold corners between layers.

robin hood/airman

(David Petty)

Start — page marker base.

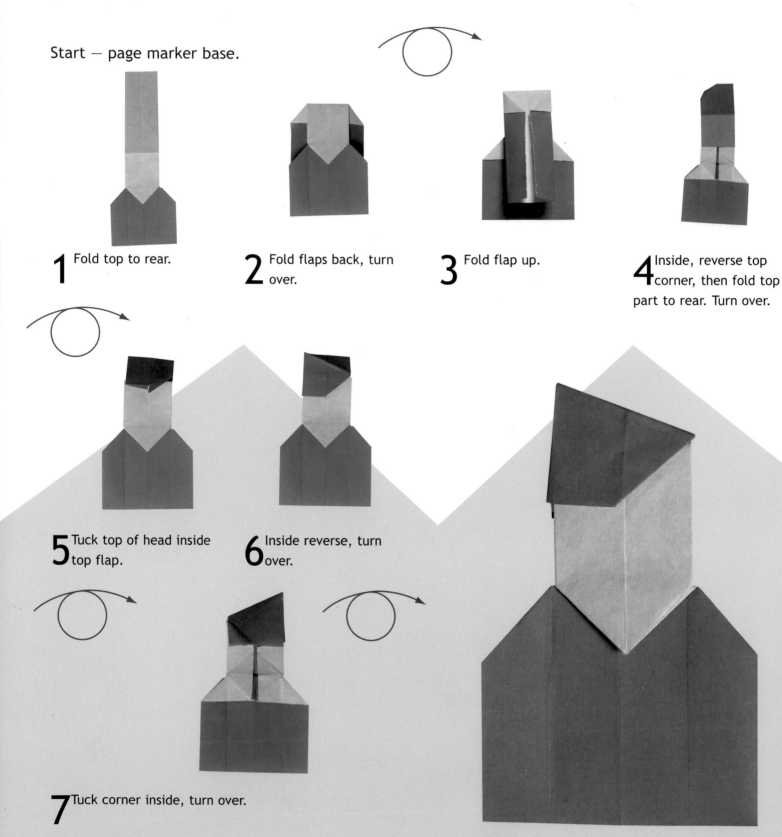

1 Fold top to rear.

2 Fold flaps back, turn over.

3 Fold flap up.

4 Inside, reverse top corner, then fold top part to rear. Turn over.

5 Tuck top of head inside top flap.

6 Inside reverse, turn over.

7 Tuck corner inside, turn over.

chef

(David Petty)

Start — pagemarker base, color reversed.

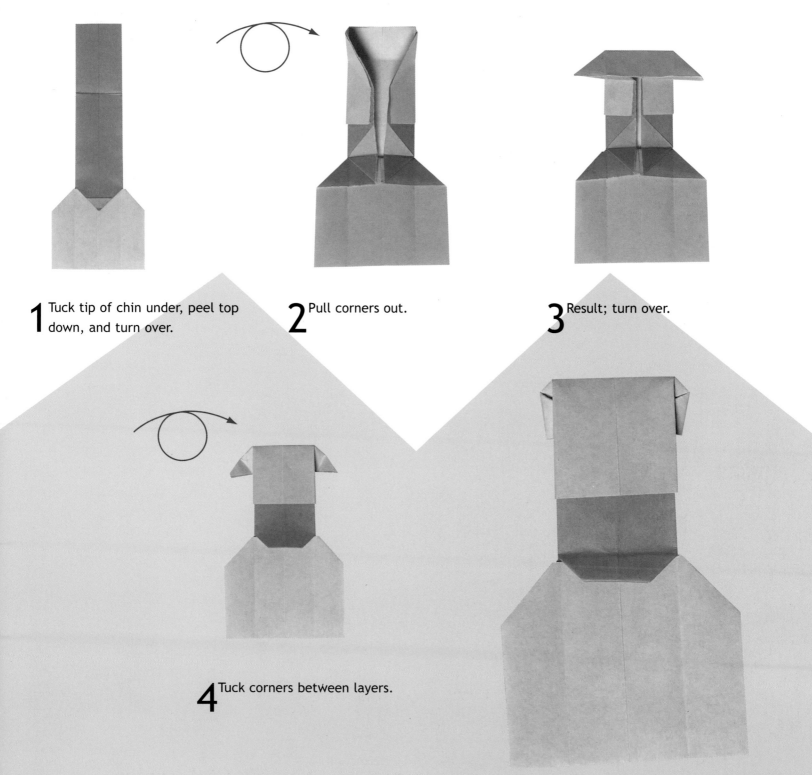

1 Tuck tip of chin under, peel top down, and turn over.

2 Pull corners out.

3 Result; turn over.

4 Tuck corners between layers.

eccentric page marker base

(David Petty)

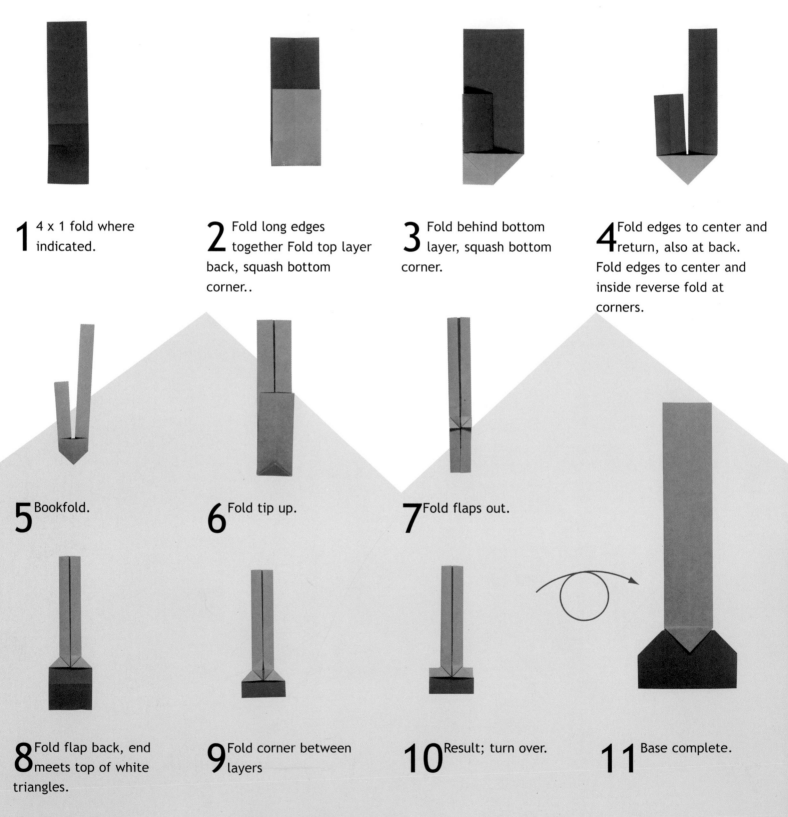

1 4 x 1 fold where indicated.

2 Fold long edges together Fold top layer back, squash bottom corner..

3 Fold behind bottom layer, squash bottom corner.

4 Fold edges to center and return, also at back. Fold edges to center and inside reverse fold at corners.

5 Bookfold.

6 Fold tip up.

7 Fold flaps out.

8 Fold flap back, end meets top of white triangles.

9 Fold corner between layers

10 Result; turn over.

11 Base complete.

the whole man

(David Petty)

Start — eccentric pagemarker base.

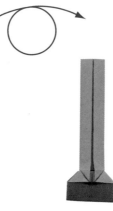

1 Fold tip under.

2 Result, turn over.

3 Open out top flaps and squash at bottom.

4 Fold top down and corners inside.

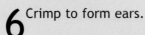

5 Fold sides to center.

6 Crimp to form ears.

7 Result, turn over.

chinaman page marker

(David Petty)

1 4 x 1 crease center, fold top quarter to rear.

2 Form waterbomb double thickness.

3 Fold flap up.

4 Fold down at half height of waterbomb.

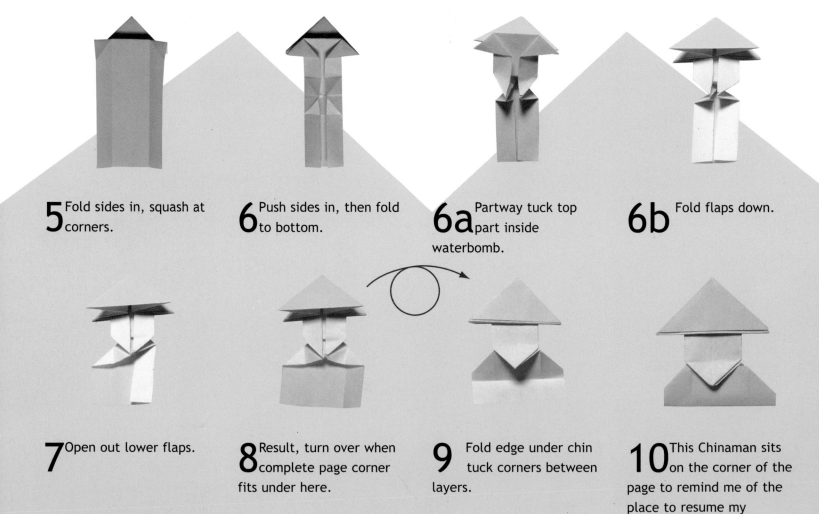

5 Fold sides in, squash at corners.

6 Push sides in, then fold to bottom.

6a Partway tuck top part inside waterbomb.

6b Fold flaps down.

7 Open out lower flaps.

8 Result, turn over when complete page corner fits under here.

9 Fold edge under chin tuck corners between layers.

10 This Chinaman sits on the corner of the page to remind me of the place to resume my reading.

pen

(David Petty)

Use 4x1 strip — foil is good.

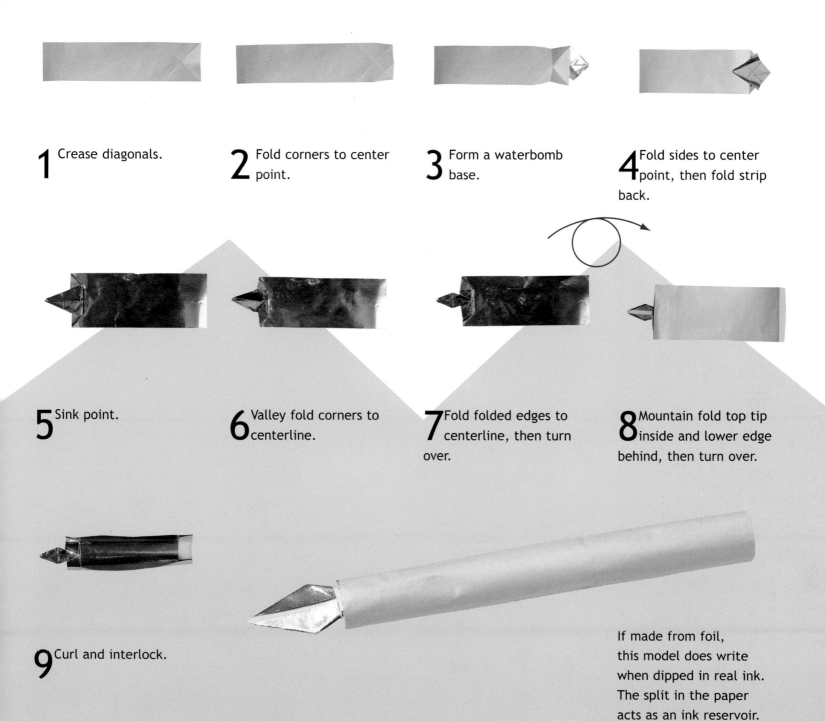

1 Crease diagonals.

2 Fold corners to center point.

3 Form a waterbomb base.

4 Fold sides to center point, then fold strip back.

5 Sink point.

6 Valley fold corners to centerline.

7 Fold folded edges to centerline, then turn over.

8 Mountain fold top tip inside and lower edge behind, then turn over.

9 Curl and interlock.

If made from foil, this model does write when dipped in real ink. The split in the paper acts as an ink reservoir.

60º star unit

(David Petty)

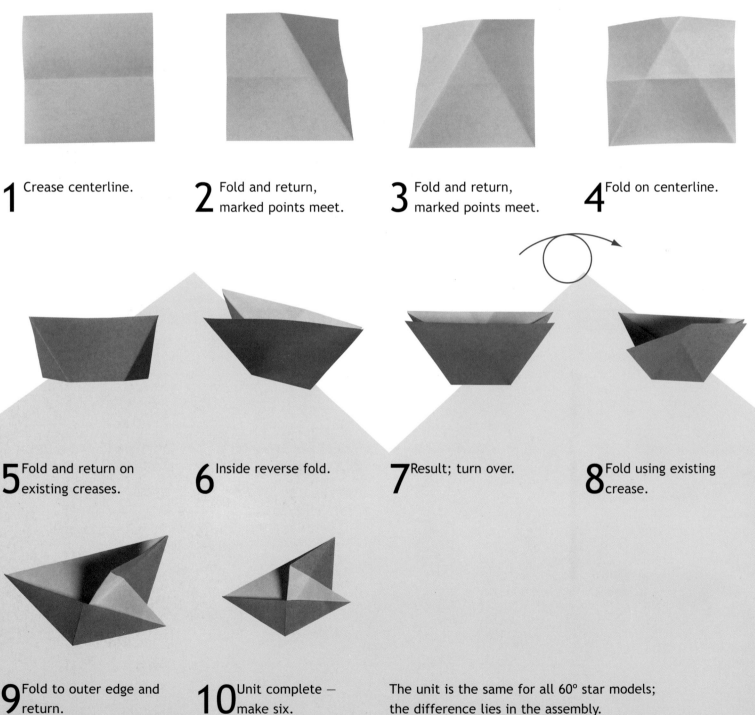

1 Crease centerline.

2 Fold and return, marked points meet.

3 Fold and return, marked points meet.

4 Fold on centerline.

5 Fold and return on existing creases.

6 Inside reverse fold.

7 Result; turn over.

8 Fold using existing crease.

9 Fold to outer edge and return.

10 Unit complete — make six.

The unit is the same for all 60º star models; the difference lies in the assembly.

60° star 1

Assembly

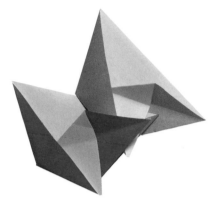

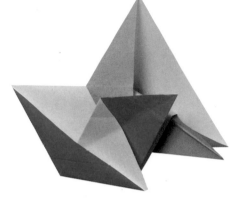

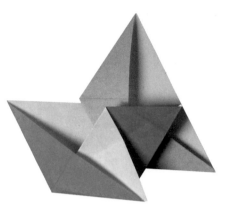

A Rear flap of left unit goes behind front flap of right unit; marked points meet.

B Fold flap on existing crease.

C Two units joined; all six join similarly.

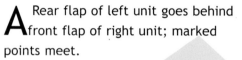

Back of star.

Variation 1

fold points over edge behind

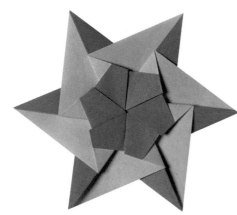

Front.

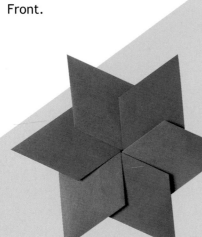

Back.

Variation 2

Make the creases one by one, then fold all tips simultaneously.

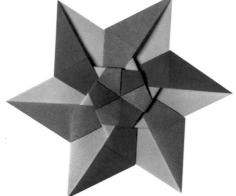

Front.

Back.

Variation 3

Start with variation 2. Fold points over edge behind.

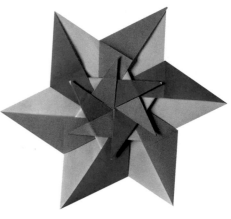

Front.

Back.

60º star 2

Assembly

A Flap on left unit goes behind flap on right unit. Marked points meet.

B Fold flap behind inner layers using existing creases.

3 Two units joined — all six to join similarly.

4 Result; fold tips behind.

bells

(David Petty)

Start — preliminary base.

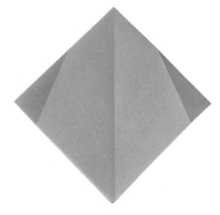

1 Fold so folded edge is parallel to centerline.

2 Unfold corners, tuck one between layers.

3 Slide/rotate sideways. The sideways motion is limited by a hidden flap.

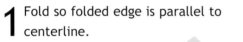

4 First, refold side corners, then tuck the tip inside, and turn over.

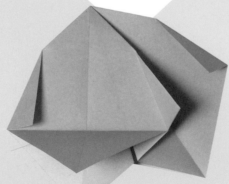

5 Refold the corner, then fold tip up.

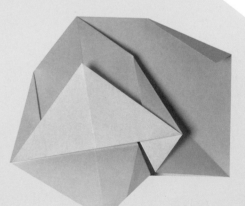

6 Tuck tip inside, squash on right.

7 Tuck tip inside, leaving point as clapper.

8 Swing flap across.

9 Tuck tip inside, leaving point as clapper.

10 Blunt points; tuck in white triangle.

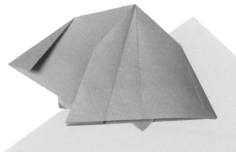

11 Turn over.

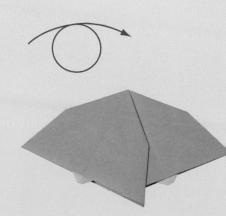

12 Complete.

Intended for use on a greetings card.

container

(David Petty)

Start — preliminary base.

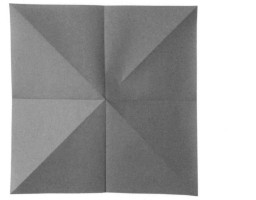

1 Precrease waterbomb base.

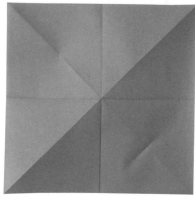

2 Mark quarter diagonals.

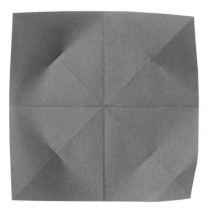

3 Mark eighth diagonals.

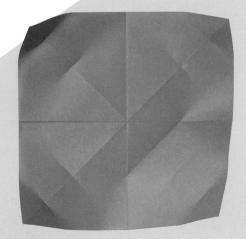

4 Fold each quadrant.

5 Fold each quadrant then turn over.

6 Pinch centers of two adjacent sides, raising central square, then work around other sides.

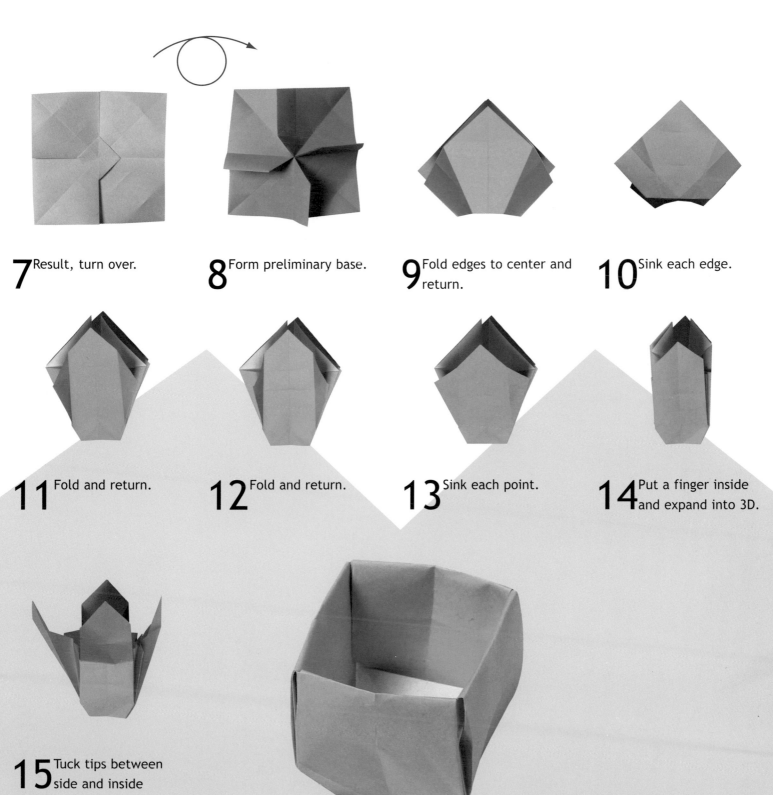

7 Result, turn over.

8 Form preliminary base.

9 Fold edges to center and return.

10 Sink each edge.

11 Fold and return.

12 Fold and return.

13 Sink each point.

14 Put a finger inside and expand into 3D.

15 Tuck tips between side and inside square.

ring of fire

(David Petty)

1 Fold diagonal.

2 Pinch only.

3 Fold corner to pinchmark, crease then return.

4 Inside reverse fold.

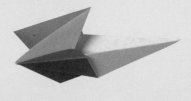

5 Fold sides down.

6 Fold back edge to top edge, repeat at rear.

7 Fold front flap over folded edge and tuck between layers. Make eight.

Assembly

  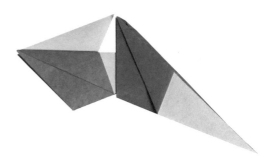

A Tuck flap of one unit into pocket of another — marked points meet.

B Fold central flap between layers.

C Fold rear flap over central flap and tuck between layers.

D Two units joined and the rest join in the same way.

wheel of fire

(David Petty)

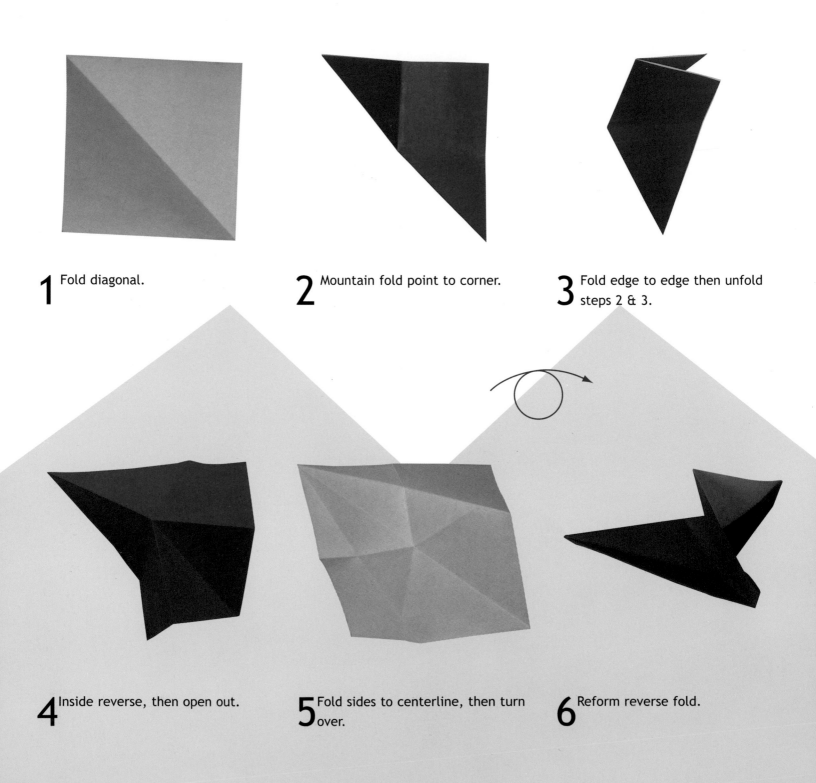

1 Fold diagonal.

2 Mountain fold point to corner.

3 Fold edge to edge then unfold steps 2 & 3.

4 Inside reverse, then open out.

5 Fold sides to centerline, then turn over.

6 Reform reverse fold.

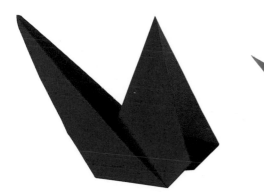

7 Make 16.

8 Tuck layers of right unit in pockets of left unit; marked points meet.

9 Valley fold tip and tuck between layers of right unit; marked points meet.

10 Join the remaining units in the same way.

Front.

Reverse.

modular construction

(David Petty)

The modular pieces "ring of fire" and "wheel of fire" can be combined provided they are both folded from the same size paper.

Simply locate "ring of fire" inside "wheel of fire." Glue is not required .

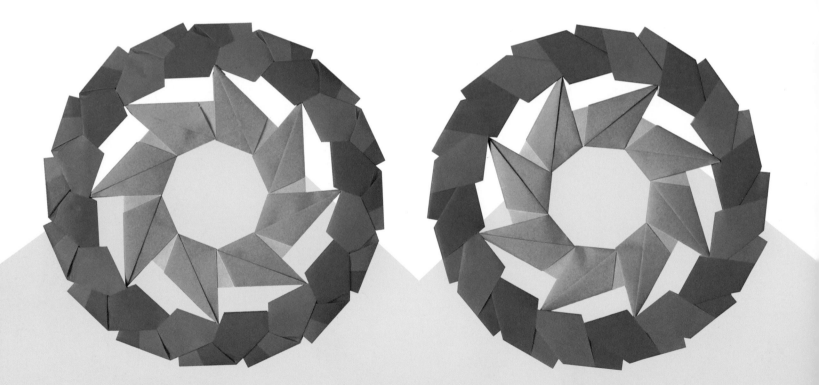

Inner Ring of Fire
Outer Wheel of Fire

olympian love

(David Petty)

Start with a 4 x 1 strip.

1 Crease quarters, pleat.

2 Fold corners to centerline.

3 Fold right edge to colored edge and return, then turn over.

4 Crease top corners and fold lower flap down.

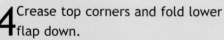

5 Inside reverse left corners, valley fold right flap.

6 Make folds then open out fully.

7 Precrease.

8 Precrease.

9 Precrease at top, valley lower edge.

10 Fold in half.

11 Make crease, then open fully.

 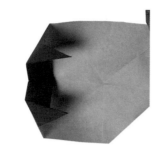 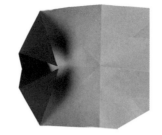 

12 Fold up lower edge, putting in folds on existing creases. Bottom part is 3D from here on.

13 Squash corners.

14 Fold lower portion up.

15 Mountain fold corners.

16 Fold corners in, pleat.

17 Inside reverse corners, then fold point down.

18 Fold top down and turn over.

19 Fold sides to center, rotate.

20 Fold top inside, valley fold points and turn over.

pencil holder

(David Petty)

1 Form preliminary base.

2 Fold edges to centerline, repeat at rear.

3 Fold and return edges to centerline, repeat at rear.

4 Unfold side flaps, valley fold and return lower point.

5 Double inside reverse all four flaps.

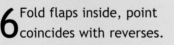

6 Fold flaps inside, point coincides with reverses.

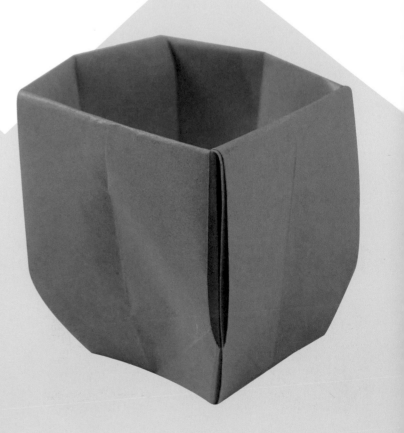

7 Tuck each flap into a pocket.

8 Put finger inside and expand to 3D, lower tip will rise and flatten.

space rocket

(David Petty)

 **1** Crease thirds.

 **2** Crease centerline.

 **3** Fold corners to centerline.

 **4** Fold on thirds line.

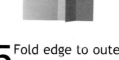 **5** Fold edge to outer edge and return.

 **6** Fold crease to outer edge.

 **7** Result; repeat steps 4-7 on left-hand side.

 **8** Result; open side flaps and convert to reverse folds.

9 Fold lower edge so it overlaps the colored paper.

 **10** Pull out side flaps.

 **11** Tuck tips inside.

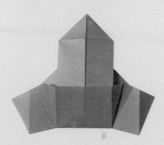 **12** Tuck flap under.

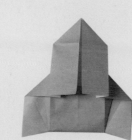 **13** Result of tuck-in. Turn over.

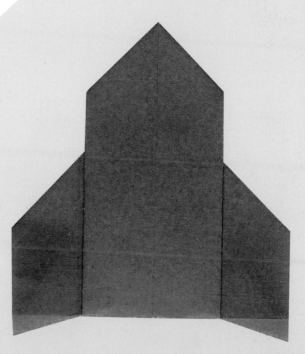

sunflower

(David Petty)

Center

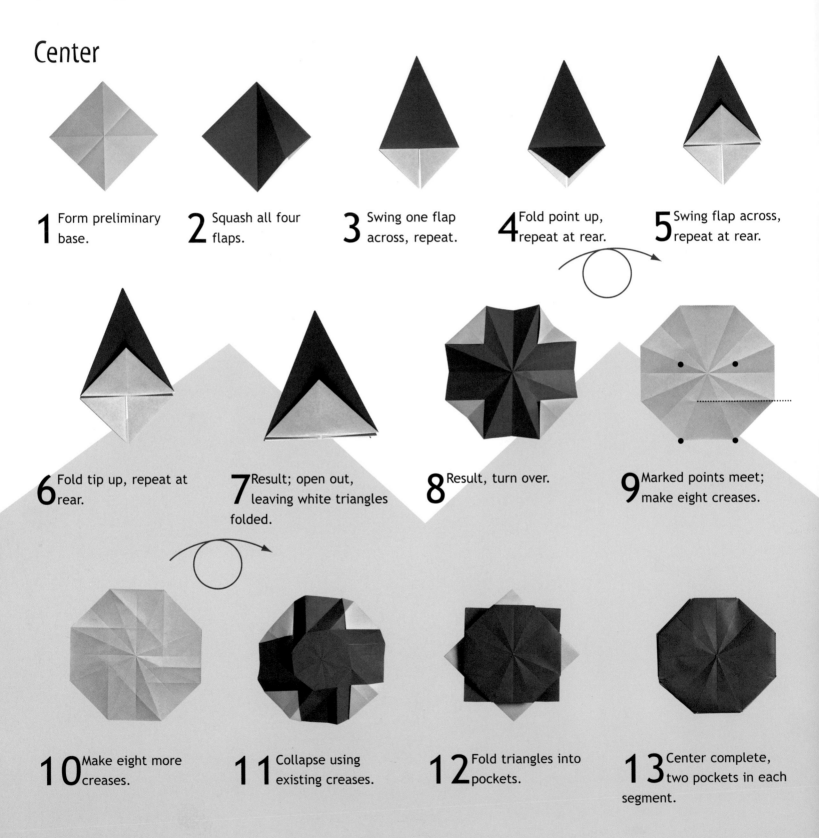

1 Form preliminary base.

2 Squash all four flaps.

3 Swing one flap across, repeat.

4 Fold point up, repeat at rear.

5 Swing flap across, repeat at rear.

6 Fold tip up, repeat at rear.

7 Result; open out, leaving white triangles folded.

8 Result, turn over.

9 Marked points meet; make eight creases.

10 Make eight more creases.

11 Collapse using existing creases.

12 Fold triangles into pockets.

13 Center complete, two pockets in each segment.

Petal

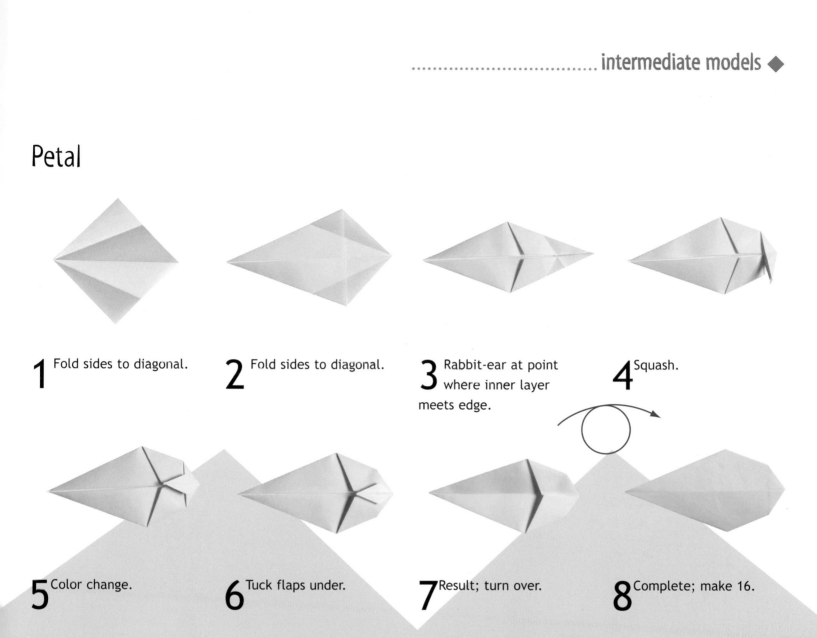

1 Fold sides to diagonal.

2 Fold sides to diagonal.

3 Rabbit-ear at point where inner layer meets edge.

4 Squash.

5 Color change.

6 Tuck flaps under.

7 Result; turn over.

8 Complete; make 16.

Assembly
Tuck petals into pockets in center. Two variations are possible.

I made my sunflower from 2¹⁄₃x 2¹⁄₃ in. (yellow) petals.and 4 x 4 in. (black or brown) center. Do you want leaves? Then fold as petal in green. Don't like sunflowers?

Then fold white petals with a yellow or red center. You then have a daisy.

Fold a center from a large sheet. Use it either way up as a coaster. **Variation** — at step 8 fold corners below.

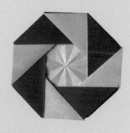

tree

(David Petty)

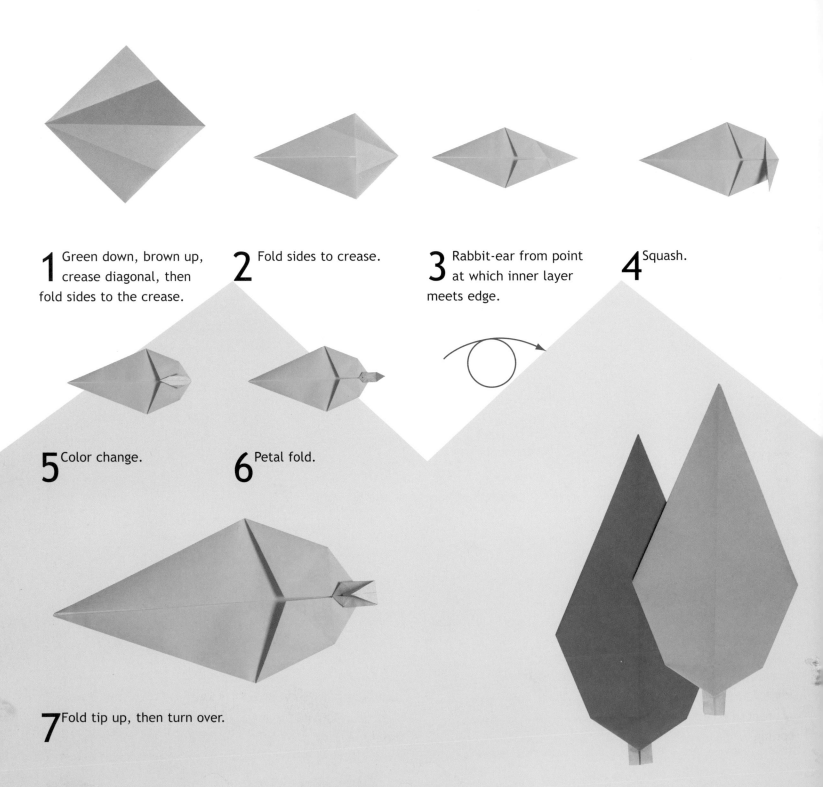

1 Green down, brown up, crease diagonal, then fold sides to the crease.

2 Fold sides to crease.

3 Rabbit-ear from point at which inner layer meets edge.

4 Squash.

5 Color change.

6 Petal fold.

7 Fold tip up, then turn over.

american jumping frog

(Traditional)

1 Form waterbomb base.

2 Fold sides to center.

3 Fold sides to folded edge.

4 Result, turn over.

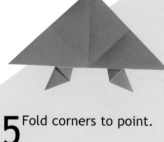

5 Fold corners to point.

6 Fold corners to side points.

7 Fold corners to make feet pleat to form spring.

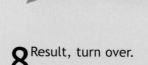

8 Result, turn over.

Complete.
To operate — run finger down the frog's back

turkish slippers

(David Petty)

Uses A4 sheet folded then cut in half.

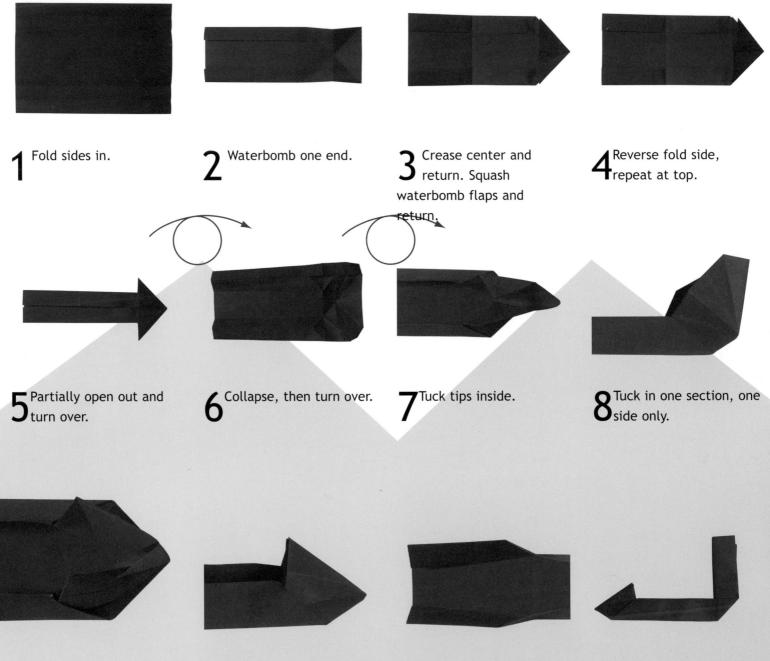

1 Fold sides in.

2 Waterbomb one end.

3 Crease center and return. Squash waterbomb flaps and return.

4 Reverse fold side, repeat at top.

5 Partially open out and turn over.

6 Collapse, then turn over.

7 Tuck tips inside.

8 Tuck in one section, one side only.

9 Bring paper across and down, one side only. Fold tip behind.

10 Tuck tip under layer behind.

11 Raise rear portion.

12 Fold sides flat to rear.

13 Fold flap down.

14 Showing creases.

15 Tuck flap inside triangular pockets.

16 Reverse fold corners and round back.

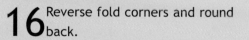

Complete.
Make the other half of the pair from the remainder of the sheet.

xyz diamonds

(David Petty)

1 Crease centerline.

2 Fold sides close to center; leave a tiny gap between the edges at the center.

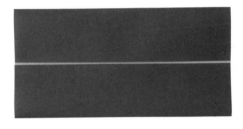

3 Result; turn over.

4 Crease at center.

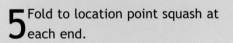

5 Fold to location point squash at each end.

6 Repeat steps 4 & 5 on other end.

7 Fold in half.

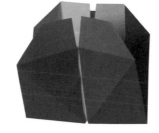

8 Inside reverses.

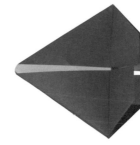

9 Fold flaps at right angles.

10 Unit complete. Make six (best with two papers of each, with three different colors).

Assembly

Tuck flaps into pockets of neighboring unit.

Continue adding units in the same way.

Assembling the first four units is easy; last two are difficult.

Altering the starting paper proportions gives different sized "planes."

basket with handles

(Traditional)

basket

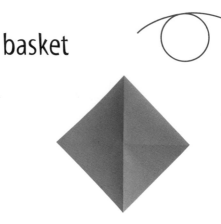

1 Crease diagonals, turn over.

2 Crease centerlines, turn over.

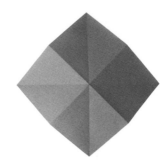

3 Form preliminary base.

4 Fold flaps down, front and back.

5 Fold tip to edge, front and back.

6 Result; add handle.

Note: handle touches white top flaps and tucks inside lower colored triangular flaps

handle

1 Fold sides to center . . .

2 . . . and again.

3 Fold in half.

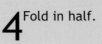

4 Fold in half.

5 Fold edge to center, folding handle too, front and back.

6 Fold corners inside to center.

7 Fold flaps down.

8 3D basket part.

9 Round handle at top, fold side flaps inside.

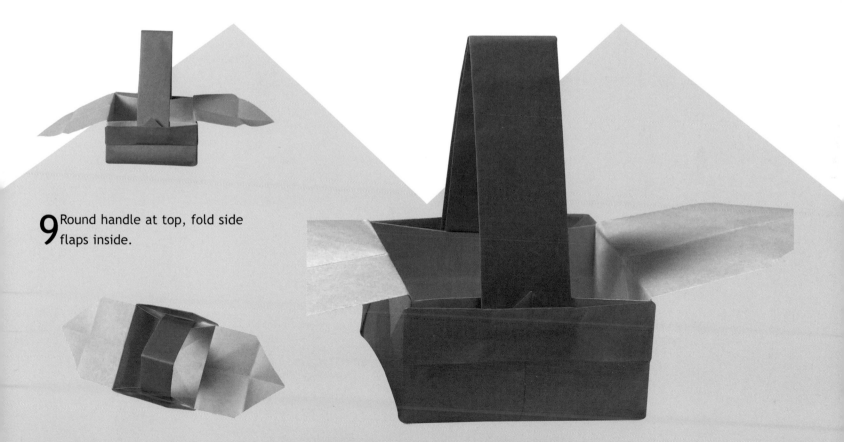

Top view.

bird

(Edwin Corrie)

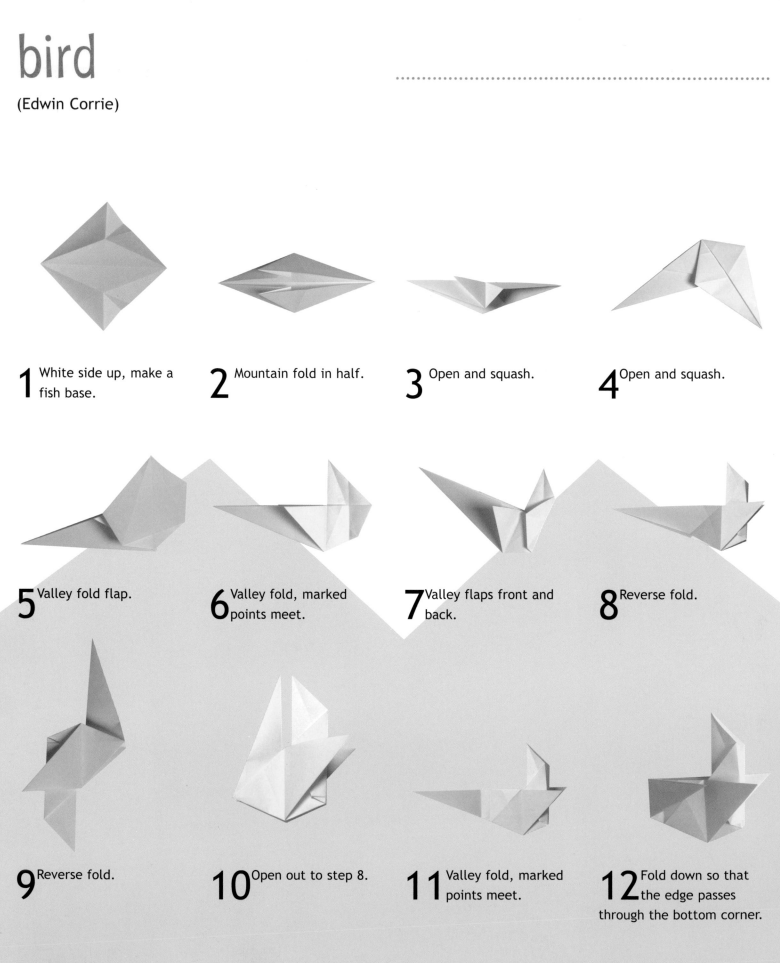

1 White side up, make a fish base.

2 Mountain fold in half.

3 Open and squash.

4 Open and squash.

5 Valley fold flap.

6 Valley fold, marked points meet.

7 Valley flaps front and back.

8 Reverse fold.

9 Reverse fold.

10 Open out to step 8.

11 Valley fold, marked points meet.

12 Fold down so that the edge passes through the bottom corner.

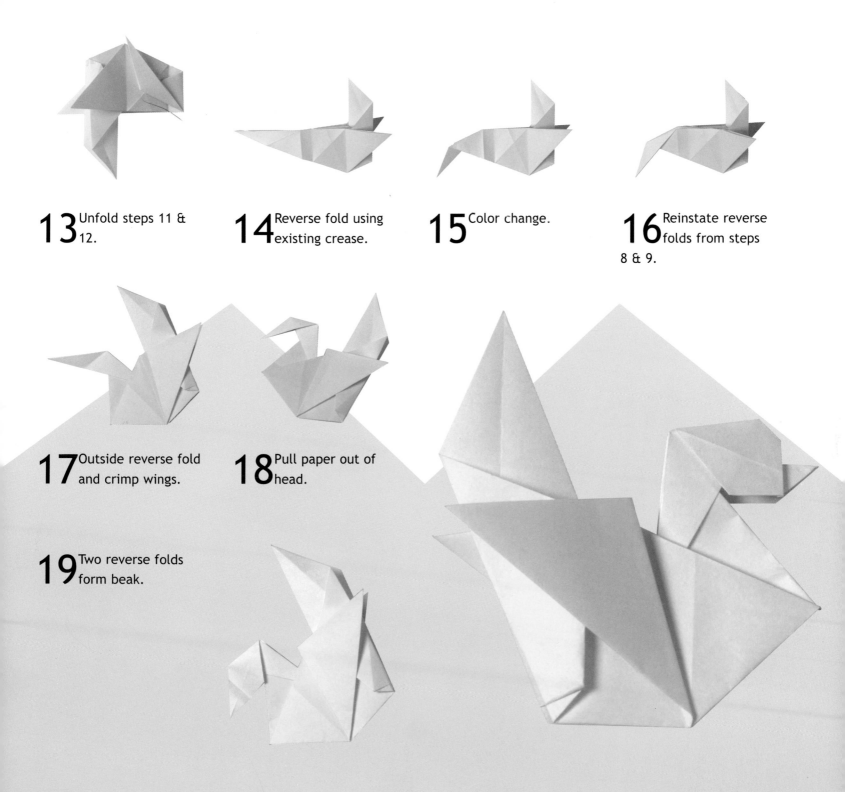

13 Unfold steps 11 & 12.

14 Reverse fold using existing crease.

15 Color change.

16 Reinstate reverse folds from steps 8 & 9.

17 Outside reverse fold and crimp wings.

18 Pull paper out of head.

19 Two reverse folds form beak.

4 advanced projects

These are the most detailed models,

which need time and understanding.

They are intended for practiced folders.

wxyz modular

(Tung Ken Lam)

Make 12 units; the best effect is when each triangle in the final model is of a different color. For this use three units in each of four different colors.

1 Pinch in center and lower edge.

2 Creases here only. Unfold to white side up.

3 Pinch quarter mark at edge.

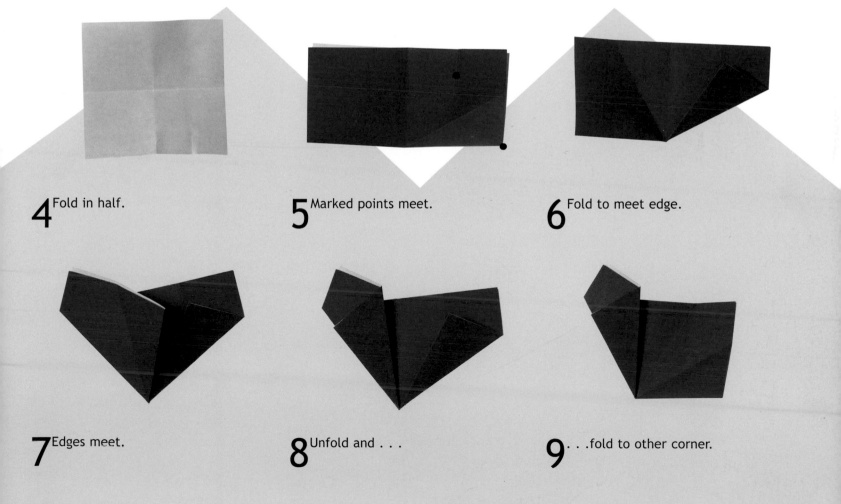

4 Fold in half.

5 Marked points meet.

6 Fold to meet edge.

7 Edges meet.

8 Unfold and . . .

9 . . .fold to other corner.

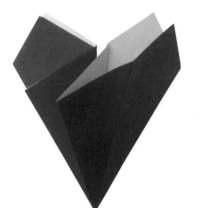

10 Squash.

11 Fold to back.

12 Unfold.

13 Squash.

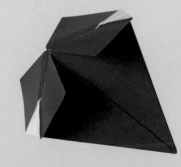

14 Fold to back.

15 Fold flaps along raw edge (repeat at back).

16 Lift flaps to stand at right angles.

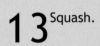

17 Make 12 units.

Assembly

Flaps in one unit go inside pocket in next unit.

Assembly can be tricky (you can get lost) and the best method is to join four units in a ring, then extend each color into a triangle.

octahedral cross

(Tung Ken Lam)

1 Crease quarter lines.

2 Crease diagonal only in central sections. Fold sides to centerline. Mountain fold along existing crease.

3 Fold inwards to center.

4 Make folds at right angles.

5 Make 12. The best effect is with four units of each of three different colors.

Assembly

Tuck flap of unit into pocket in second unit.

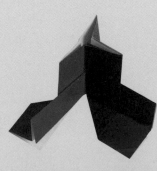

Two units joined, others join similarly.

Assembly is best done with the aid of paper clips!

pineapple

(David Petty)

Start with orange and brown paper.

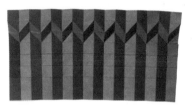
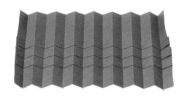

1 Precrease into sixteenths.

2 Fold top 2/16th behind, and make pleats at 3rd, 6th and 9th creases.

3 Pleat, valley-mountain etc.

4 Reverse folds.

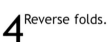

5 Side view of result of step 4. Curl ends round.

6 Interlock layers, and overlap every second 16th

7 Inside reverse crease bottom corner.

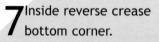

8 Fold up bottom flaps to lock base. Shape by stretching the sides.

tensegrity module variation

(Ian Harrison)

Make 12 units; the best effect is when each triangle in the final model is of a different color: for this use three units in each of four different colors.

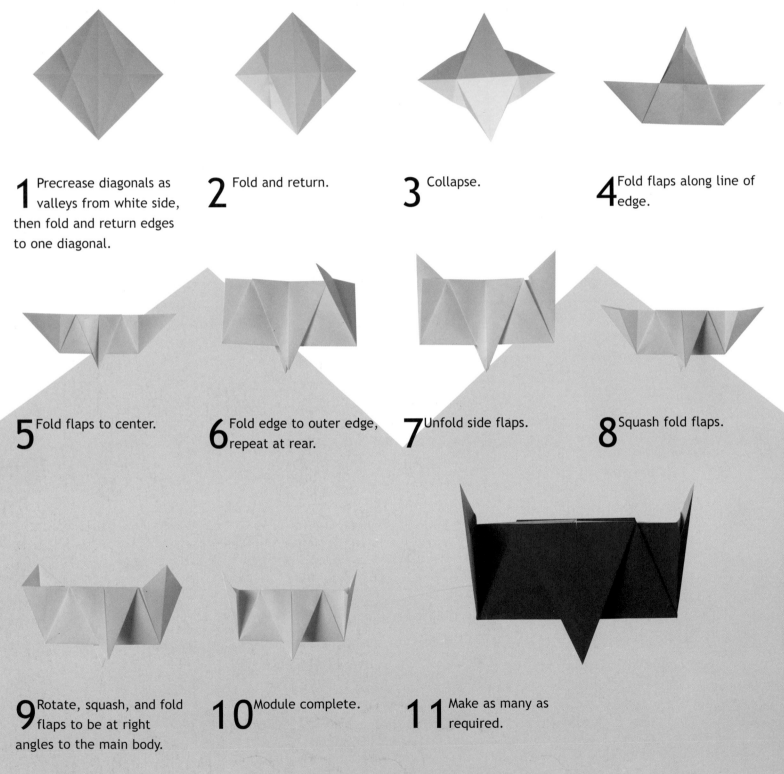

1 Precrease diagonals as valleys from white side, then fold and return edges to one diagonal.

2 Fold and return.

3 Collapse.

4 Fold flaps along line of edge.

5 Fold flaps to center.

6 Fold edge to outer edge, repeat at rear.

7 Unfold side flaps.

8 Squash fold flaps.

9 Rotate, squash, and fold flaps to be at right angles to the main body.

10 Module complete.

11 Make as many as required.

Assembly

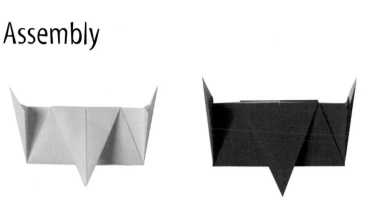

One flap of right module tucks into pocket of left module.

Two modules joined.
Remainder join similarly.

Variation

This variation can be used for polyhedra where four edges meet at a vertex, such as the octahedron, the cuboctahedron, and the icosidodecahedron.

For the cuboctahedron (12 modules), each half of each module is common to a triangle and a square, with triangles and squares alternately round a vertex (the center of the module). Similarly, for the icosidodecahedron (30 modules) the faces are triangles and pentagons alternately at the center of a module.

The clever module design is by Ian Harrison. Whilst folding his modular pieces, I came across a surprise. Expecting to produce a regular prism, I discovered a twisted piece which I dubbed "maypole", because of the twist and the colors. This piece has also been called "stack-o-stars".

51 modules
Start at one end with a ring of three modules, add further modules, with alternate rings of four and three to form an end cap. The body is formed from rings of four, complete with end cap in mirror image. End caps are half cuboctahedrons.

The twist comes naturally and does not have to be encouraged.

120° unit

(Ian Harrison)

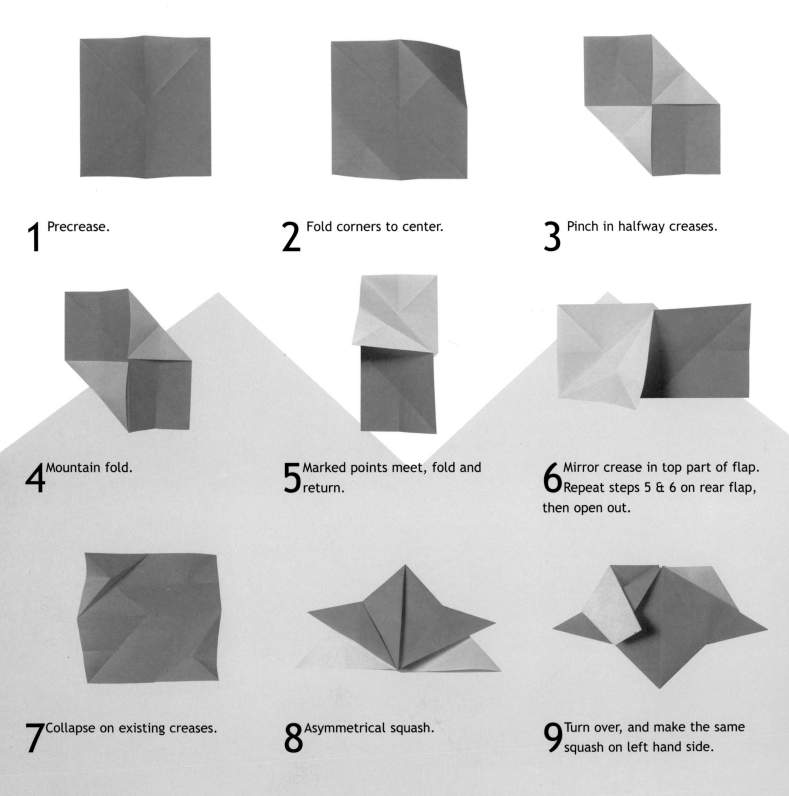

1 Precrease.

2 Fold corners to center.

3 Pinch in halfway creases.

4 Mountain fold.

5 Marked points meet, fold and return.

6 Mirror crease in top part of flap. Repeat steps 5 & 6 on rear flap, then open out.

7 Collapse on existing creases.

8 Asymmetrical squash.

9 Turn over, and make the same squash on left hand side.

Assembly

Joining the units together leaves a white triangle on the right within the triangular dimples when using standard origami paper.

10 Rotate squashed flaps to 90°.

Start with a ring of three units, then extend each unit into a six-pointed star plane. A fourth plane (blue in the illustration) is added halfway. Each triangular ring is surrounded by four unit rings.

The model is based on a cuboctahedron, and has four six-point star planes. Paper clips are useful to stabilize the structure during assembly.

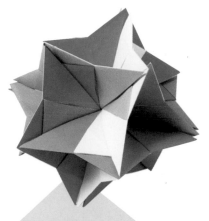

11 Unit complete; make 12.

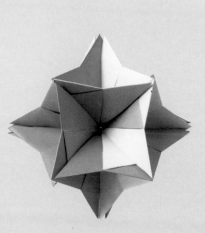

90º unit

(Ian Harrison)

1 Mountain fold.

2 Fold corners to center.

3 Mountain fold.

4 Rabbit-ear fold and return. Repeat on rear flap, then open out.

5 Collapse on existing creases.

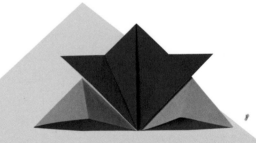

6 Squashes.

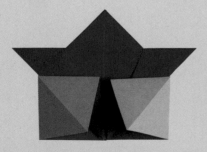

7 Rotate squash flaps to 90°.

8 Unit complete; make 20.

Assembly

Flaps of right unit tuck into pockets in left unit.

Two units joined; all 20 join similarly.

White shows on right within some rings, when using standard origami paper.

Start with a ring of five units, each a different color. Extend each side into a ring of three units to make another similar ring with extended sides (using a reversed direction of joining). Join the two structures, one upside down, to the other, to give five eight-point star planes.

The model is very loosely based on pentagonal anti-prism ring. The structure is:-

5
33333
44444
44444
33333
5

Paper clips are useful to stabilize the structure during assembly.

rota cup

(David Petty)

1 Crease centerlines.

2 Mountain fold on third lines.

3 Add valley folds to third lines.

4 Mountain fold central square and raise center.

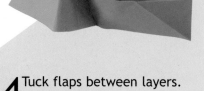

4 Tuck flaps between layers.

5 Turn over.

Complete. This is an example of twist folding.

borealis variation

(David Petty)

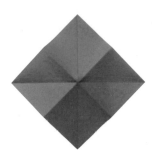

1 Form preliminary base.

2 Fold sides to center and return.

3 Sink top point.

4 Fold point to center of top edge, repeat on all four sides.

5 Swing front flap to other side.

6 Decorated unit one complete. Make 30 (or 24 or 18).

6a For plain unit, tuck triangles under.

6b Plain unit complete make 30 (or 24 or 18).

6c For alternative decorated unit, fold edges of white triangles behind.

6d Decorated unit two complete. Make 30 (or 24 or 18).

6e For alternative decorated unit, fold only one edge of white triangles behind.

6f Decorative unit three complete. Make 30 (or 24 or 18).

Assembly

(same principle for all units)

A Tuck one flap inside the other.

B Fold tip at right angle.

C Two units joined.

Join the units, starting with a ring of five to form a sunken pentagon. One unit is added to each of the two arms at the corners to give small triangles. Eventually each side of the triangles forms part of another pentagon. Pay attention to the white areas. Best results are when all units within each pentagon are similar. Unlike borealis, this modular piece is skeletal and patterned, which makes it more dynamic

Here's a selection of completed models using the different units, including color reversal of units. Constructions are from 30, 24 or 18 units.

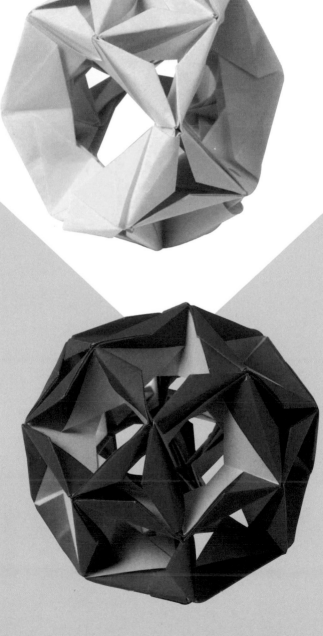

chinese vase

(traditional)

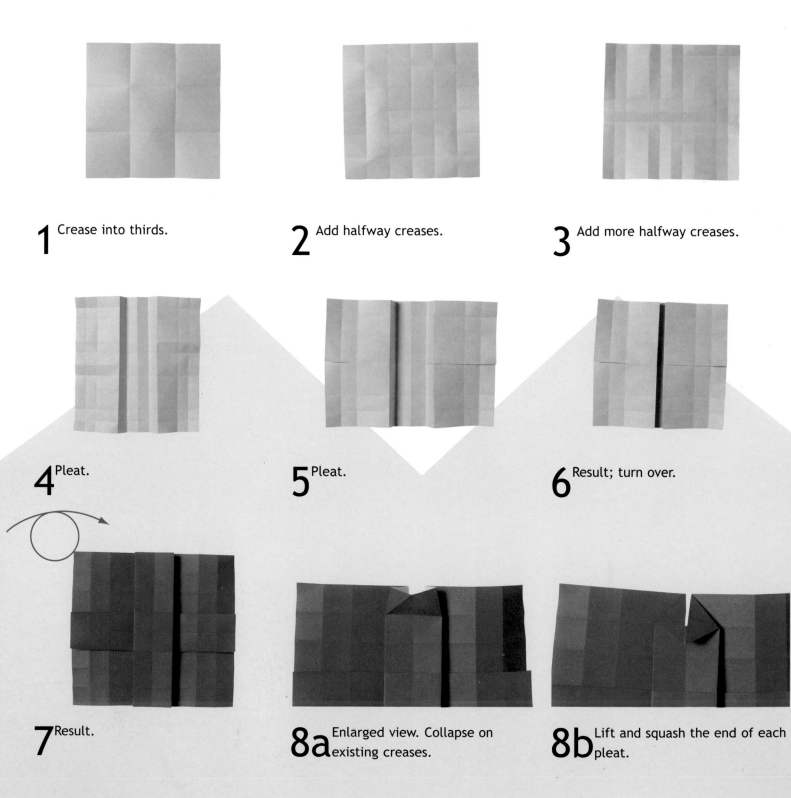

1 Crease into thirds.

2 Add halfway creases.

3 Add more halfway creases.

4 Pleat.

5 Pleat.

6 Result; turn over.

7 Result.

8a Enlarged view. Collapse on existing creases.

8b Lift and squash the end of each pleat.

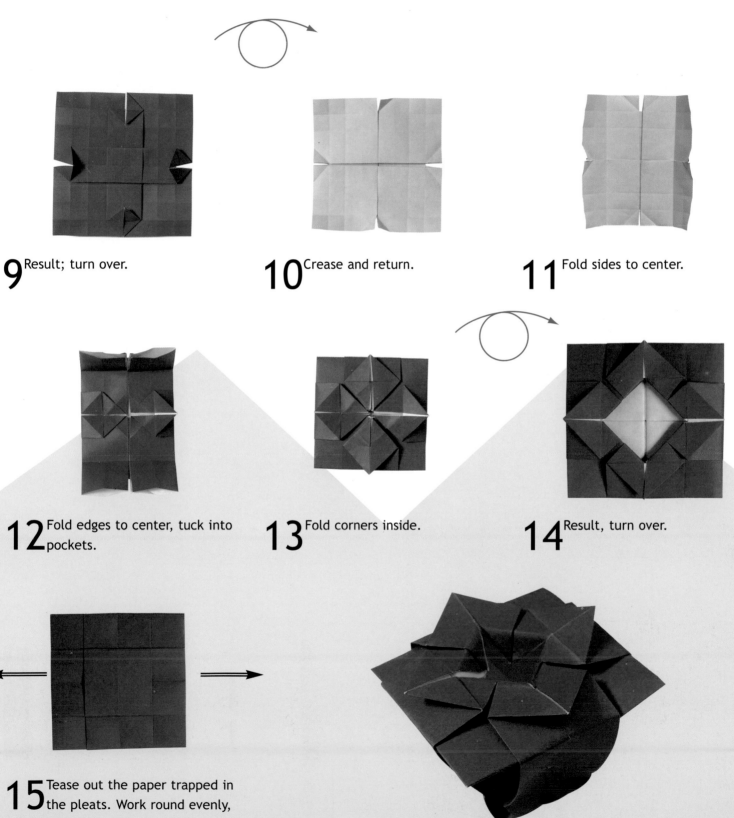

9 Result; turn over.

10 Crease and return.

11 Fold sides to center.

12 Fold edges to center, tuck into pockets.

13 Fold corners inside.

14 Result, turn over.

15 Tease out the paper trapped in the pleats. Work round evenly, a little at a time.

3d christmas tree

(David Petty)

1 Precrease into eighteenths.

2 Pleat as indicated.

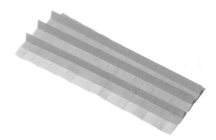

3 Fold edges down in order. Produce points where marked P follows steps 4-6.

4 Form a pleat, then unfold and reform while pushing top edge down and pulling bottom edge forward. Picture shows this partway.

5 Point complete.

6 Unfold all points to return to step 4. Pleat, then curl ends together.

7 Interweave and overlap 2/18ths. Re-form pleats to form eight fluted columns.

8 Refold the points from steps 5–7. Fold top tips inside.

 index

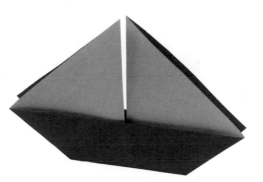

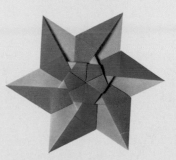

credits & acknowledgments

GUEST CREATORS

Acknowledgment is given to the following creators who gave permission for their work to be included in this book.

Tun Ken Lam — British, with a mathematical bent, his modular creations are fine examples of original and economical folding.

Ian Harrison — British, also with highly developed mathematical side, his creations tend to be geometric.

Ibolya Tuzy — Hungarian, she too demonstrates originality and economy in her models.

Edwin Corrie — British, known for animal models.

PAPER

Most models in this book are designed to use standard origami paper which is colored one side and white on the other. The final model will demonstrate if the white side of the paper is designed to show. Some models will turn out fine using paper the same color both sides. My advice is to use the cheapest paper you can find (brown paper, copier paper, wrapping paper, newspaper etc.) when folding a model for the first time. If it goes badly wrong, then not much is lost. When you have learned the model, then use the more expensive paper.

There are extensive ranges of origami paper available. Ranging from Japanese washi (expensive), through patterned and foiled papers (less expensive), to plain color and duo colored paper (less expensive still). Packs of paper intended for modular work are available, usually in smaller sizes, with many sheets of the same color. Beware of patterned papers — it can sometimes be hard to see the creases required to fold the model correctly.

There are several internet sources of paper too - auction sites as well as book sellers.

SOCIETIES

Folders who would like to join a society are advised to contact the following :

British Origami Society
http://www.britishorigami.org.uk/

Origami USA
http://www.origami-usa.org/

David Petty maintains a website at the URL :

http://members.aol.com/ukpetd/

where instructions for many traditional and contemporary models can be found.

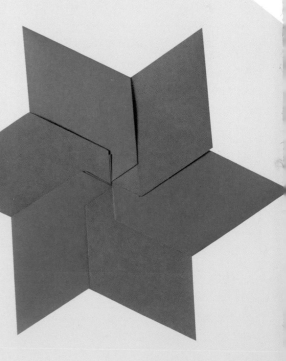